Traveling with Children and Enjoying It

Traveling with Children and Enjoying It

A Complete Guide to Family Travel by Car, Plane, and Train

By Arlene Kay Butler

A Voyager Book

The Globe Pequot Press

Chester, Connecticut

Photographs by Timothy J. Connolly,
except photograph page xiii by Kathryn M. Lewis

Library of Congress Cataloging-in -Publication Data

Butler, Arlene Kay.
  Traveling with children and enjoying it : a complete guide to family travel by car, plane, and train / by Arlene Kay Butler. — 1st ed.
    p. cm.
    Includes index.
    ISBN 0-87106-316-6
    1. Travel. 2. Children—Care and hygiene. 3. Family recreation.
I. Title.
G151.B88   1991
649'.5—dc20   90-28547
                                                            CIP

        649.5

Manufactured in the United States of America
First Edition/First Printing

6498

C

To the people in my life who have believed in me, especially my parents and my husband.

Table of Contents

Introduction

We were off—the first day of another memorable trip. Our four-year-old had already spilled orange juice on the baby as we attempted to eat breakfast in the car to save time. Our six-year-old had whined nonstop for two hours, and the others had kept busy by pinching each other. I knew they would soon begin to ask, "Mom, when will we get there?" I had a headache and had already resorted to threats.

A typical family outing? Yes and no. Children are usually marvelous traveling companions, eager to explore new surroundings and open to adventures. Their energy and enthusiasm is contagious, and parents are drawn into their fresh outlook on such "ordinary" experiences as a ferry ride, room service, or a glass elevator. Of course, traveling families still must cope with many of the same issues they face at home, and when children get bored and irritable frustrated parents wonder what possessed them to venture out with their offspring.

Traveling with Children and Enjoying It—A Complete Guide to Family Travel by Car, Plane, and Train is designed to keep families happily organized and entertained before, during, and after vacations and other adventures away from home. It is a comprehensive book with practical advice and tips for planning a vacation, packing, anticipating costs, predicting the needs of all members of the family, and smoothing the rough edges of new experiences. It includes advice on how to cope with long automobile trips, plane flights, and train rides. Parents will be better prepared to handle health and safety considerations, discipline, mealtimes, bedtimes, and much more. Chapters with activities, games, and songs make *Traveling with Children* an ideal take-along book, and the final chapter even helps families adjust to returning home. You may photocopy the handy checklists found throughout the book.

The Family That Travels Together

Traveling as a family is a terrific opportunity to draw your family closer together. Family vacations strengthen the ties of parent to child, and sibling to sibling, as you share happy experiences and create wonderful memories that will last your lifetimes.

Vacations provide a good chance to talk, listen, and express your love and interest. You can really get to know and enjoy each other without the distractions found at home. The stresses of modern family life can be greatly relieved by a vacation where all members are part of an experience of discovery, adventure, or even just plain rest and relaxation.

Put aside your worries about giving *things* to your children, and remember to give them the more precious gift of yourselves. Use travel to spend time with your children, play with them, talk with them, teach them, and love them. Share yourself and what's important to you, and you will return home with much more than an armload of souvenirs.

Discover the Magic

In addition to encouraging the flowering of family relationships, the change of pace during a family vacation stimulates curiosity and discovery. Travel broadens chil-

The author and her family

dren's horizons and usually proves to be educational as
well as therapeutic.

A trip with children also enriches the experiences of
parents. As adults we forget to see the world as we did
when we were children. Kids see and appreciate what
adults miss or take for granted. Their excitement and

appreciation for life will color your experience as well. Welcome their joy and exuberance into your travels and you will soon marvel at a renewed view of the world through a child's eyes.

You'll discover and know the world better yourself as you explain it to your children and answer their questions. It's been said, "A family vacation is like a garage sale. You never know what you'll discover."

Watch Out for Pitfalls

Family travel requires planning, organization, patience, and compromise. By planning ahead and preparing wisely (physically and mentally!), you can make family travel easy, enjoyable, and memorable. With each successive trip, you will learn more about what works best for your family; make notes so that you remember to use those ideas on subsequent vacations.

Most importantly, remember to be realistic—travel with children has limitations. At times the air will seem to ring with phrases like "I have to go potty," "I want a drink," and "Are we there yet?" We sometimes carry an unrealistic image of perfection that no mere mortal can ever match, and then we wonder why we're disappointed. Keep your expectations reasonable.

If you do run into problems, try to take them in stride and keep your sense of humor. Maintain a positive attitude and, consequently, a positive experience. Children will pick up and imitate the attitudes and feelings of parents. Don't come home from your vacation tired, frustrated, and needing a rest. A bad trip can color life at home for a while as easily as a good trip can. Certainly it would be nicer to let happy memories carry you through the days and weeks following your return.

Sharing the Journey

My own love of traveling and the desire to be able to travel successfully with my five children has led me to the research and experiences that have culminated in this book. We have traveled throughout the western United States, Mexico, and Canada. Our goal is to see all of North America, then the world!

My children include a sweet eighteen-month-old baby girl, an active three-year-old boy, an energetic, fun-loving seven-year-old (every family needs one!), a nine-year-old boy who doesn't want to go anywhere (until he gets there), and a twelve-year-old girl who is a marvelous traveler.

When we first started traveling we made mistakes. I remember one Labor Day weekend spending four hours trying to find lodging in San Francisco because we hadn't made reservations. Looking back, I wish I knew then what I do now—but I'm so glad we ventured out. It's not the problems I recall, but the beautiful memories we share together as a family. I wouldn't have missed our wonderful experiences for the world!

So what are you waiting for? There's always a reason not to go. You have the ideas and suggestions in this book to help you make your family travel exciting and rewarding. There's a big, beautiful world out there to explore— you have places to go, people to meet, and things to do! I'll see you there!

CHAPTER 1

Travel Plans

Travel Plans

How do you decide where to go, where to stay, where to eat, what to see, what to do, how to get there, and how to get around when you get there? First of all, remember you are embarking on a family vacation. You may not need to, or even want to, solicit everyone's opinion, but as you consider the choices make sure you have considered your traveling companions. Secondly, do your homework. After you've narrowed your options to two or three possibilities, gather as much factual material on the destination or activity as you can. Check travel guides, maps, lodging brochures, and other sources for the latest information to help you make a confident choice.

■ TRAVEL CHOICES ■

Once you are armed with information, choose the style in which you prefer to travel. You can go to one place or tour several points of interest. Those points may be recreational, historical, or educational, or they may involve visits to friends and family. You may want to pursue a favorite family sport, such as skiing, bicycling, or hiking. You may want to see all that you can in the time available, sightsee at a leisurely pace, or relax in one spot. Of course you have to decide whether you will have a lengthy stay or a quick jaunt, a destination many miles from home or a simple day's journey away. All these choices made, you can then choose from car, plane, train, or boat transportation.

Whatever your interests, remember to see your own part of the country. Some people have never visited nearby canyons, lakes, mountains, zoos, historical spots, or museums. These are especially good for day trips and weekends. We thought we'd live in one place forever, but when we moved, we realized we hadn't really seen our own backyard. We've been making up for it ever since!

Consider visiting state and national parks and forests, historical sites, the beach, amusement parks, ski areas, guest ranches, and family resorts. Many of the latter two options offer sports-adventure packages for parents and all but the youngest children. Popular destinations have obvious advantages and merits. They can also have crowds, noise, scarce accommodations, long lines, and delays. If it is possible for your family, travel during the less crowded off-season. It will save you time, money, and headaches.

If possible include older children in your travel decisions and planning. You might have a family council to discuss your vacation. Encourage and respect input from everyone on where they would like to go and what they want to see and do. Children are generally more willing to go along with family decisions when they've had a part in making them. Naturally, don't ask for opinions on nonnegotiable issues such as time and budget. Blend ideas, find alternatives, and try to accomplish at least some of each person's dreams while staying within your limitations.

Ask yourself these questions as you make your destination choice and plan your travel schedule:

What do we want from this trip? A change of pace, rest, solitude, activity, adventure, education, entertainment, family togetherness, a visit with friends and family? Are we looking for a pleasant combination of these options? Choose a trip that fits the interests, needs, goals, and limitations of your family. Obligations to extended family also might need to be considered.

Does this trip offer something of interest to everyone? It's a good idea to alternate adult and children's activities. If possible, let the family split off to enjoy separate activities. A reunion at day's end is often a delightful exchange of experiences enjoyed independently.

I have found that guided tours, especially of adult-oriented sights, are very difficult to do with younger children. The children cannot talk for a long period of time, and you must proceed at the tour guide's pace, which is often too slow for restless children. Furthermore, the information given is frequently geared to adults. In many such situations, it's very difficult to take care of needs such as going potty, wanting a bottle, and other urgencies. If you enjoy guided tours, select those that are geared to children. The tour of the city aquarium is probably a better choice than a tour of a winery or elegant mansion.

Do our plans respect everyone's (including the adults'!) limitations and age capabilities? Make sure the activities do not overtire, frighten, or overwhelm any one person. Large theme parks, for instance, can be hard for young or physically challenged family members. Not everyone can scuba dive or sit in the sun. Consider these issues fairly.

Are we trying to go too far in the time available? You don't want to spend your vacation barreling across the nation with no time to enjoy sights along the way. It may take two full days to recover from a twelve-hour drive even if you're simply staying put at Grandma's house.

Are we trying to do too much in the time available? Allow enough time to enjoy your discoveries. If you aren't realistic about what your family can do in a certain amount of time, your only memories may be of physical and mental exhaustion. Don't hurry past the joy and beauty. If you need to, save some sights for the next time.

Have we scheduled some leisure time or quiet days for rest and relaxation? Your trip will be less hectic if you alternate quiet and active days. Plan at least one slower-paced day for each week of travel.

Have we included private time for the adults and teenagers? Parents may want to schedule an activity or a meal away from the kids. Make babysitting arrangements before you leave home, if possible. The kids will probably enjoy a break from parental vigilance, and you *know* the wonders it will do for *your* nerves.

Have we built in some room for flexibility? If the trip's success depends on all plans going just right, you're probably overbooked or underorganized. Don't count on picking up diapers after you leave the airport if the ones you have won't last through a serious delay. Try to avoid setting up tight schedules. No matter how well *you* plan, unforeseen circumstances may force changes.

Are we organized for this trip? Check reservations, restock the first aid kit, pack for varying temperatures and weather, have maps and guidebooks on hand. Attend to as many details as possible before you set out. The better organized you are, the better your plans will fall into place.

Are our plans in keeping with our budget? If you need to, make changes to fit the family finances. You may be tempted to splurge occasionally, but don't seriously shake the piggybank unless you can afford the setback.

As you decide what you would enjoy with the time and money available, consider your options carefully and realistically, bearing in mind that the trip will be more successful if the needs and interests of the children weigh heavily in the final choice.

■ *PLANNING* ■

Planning is essential to an enjoyable trip with children. Planning will help you accommodate everyone's wishes, save time and money, reduce the potential for frustration or even disaster. Without clear plans, families may find travel difficult at best.

Two-parent families need to discuss child care and discipline, sleeping arrangements, and issues presented by your chosen mode of transportation. If you can divide these responsibilities fairly at home, you may avoid problems en route. Single parents traveling without an adult companion will need to adjust their plans accordingly.

A flexible plan will allow more freedom and enjoyment than a headlong rush out the door without a thought. It may have been high adventure to take off with a backpack and no reservations when you were on your own, but a parent, a few hungry kids, and no hotel is no fun at all.

Allow enough planning time so that the family can enjoy the excitement and anticipation of the family vacation. Children (and adults) love to look forward to a trip, discuss it, and tell their friends about it. Be careful that you don't discuss the trip so far in advance that the children will become confused or upset by the wait. You wouldn't build Christmas up in February, nor would you wait until December 23rd.

To help prepare children, make a trip countdown calendar so they can see when the trip starts and what needs to be done before you are ready to go. You can also make a countdown chain out of construction paper. Join strips of paper into a chain, making one link for each day that must pass before Day 1 of the trip. Each day the child tears off a link. A trip preparation activity can be written on each link and accomplished on a daily schedule.

Homework First

To get the most from your trip, find out about points of interest and attractions suitable for families. Talk to friends or a travel agent; read guide books, brochures, and travel articles; look at maps and contact your auto club if you are traveling by car (many clubs will help you plan your itinerary); write for information and schedules of special events from chamber of commerce and tourist offices in the vicinity of your destination.

Investigate safe and sensible routes, scenic areas, interesting activities, special events, museums, villages, festivals, and other options of interest for children, and family-oriented tours and packages. Ask for directions, recommendations on lodging, and information on anticipated delays or detours due to roadwork or weather. Collect updated information on the costs of transportation, lodging, food, and admissions.

When choosing a guidebook consider your destination, your special interests, and your budget range. Choose a book that seems to fit your program and provides maps and listings of hotels, restaurants, transportation, events, and tourist attractions. A good guidebook can tell you how to make reservations at area accommodations. Individual entries usually include the location, amenities, and rates of inns, hotels, guest homes, or motels. Some include a critique of services and overall quality. Is the book oriented to family travel? Does it list costs of cribs, babysitting services, or children's meals? Does it include sights of special interest to children? These guidebooks are especially well-suited to planning a family trip:

Birmbaum's guides
Let's Go guides
Great Vacations with Your Kids, by Dorothy Jordan & Marjorie Cohen
Places to Go with Children guides, by Chronicle Books
Recommended Family Inns, by Elizabeth Squier et al.
Recommended Family Resorts, by Jane Wilford with Janet Tice
Fielding's Family Vacations, USA by Diane Torrens
Super Family Vacations, by Martha Shirk & Nancy Klepper
Family Camping Made Simple, by Beverly Liston
In and Out of Boston (With or Without Children), by Bernice Chesler

Friends can give you information about areas the tour books may have overlooked. They may be able to share first-hand information on good and bad times to visit areas, pitfalls, lesser known attractions, good restaurants, and more. If you ask your friends about places to go, take personal taste in consideration. Some people prefer the beach, others a museum.

If you stay with friends or relatives, do your research and plan your activities as you would for any other trip. If you assume that your hosts will have everything planned, you'll probably end up bored and disappointed after a few days. Tourists often know more about a place than do the residents.

■ *TRANSPORTATION* ■

A car is the least expensive mode of travel and allows you the freedom to go at your own pace and see what you want. It is familiar and less restraining than plane travel, and needs can be taken care of with relative ease. Cars are private—a child can cry, have a diaper change, or eat without upsetting strangers. A car is slower, however, and sometimes breaks down, and an adult must always be available to drive.

A recreational vehicle (RV) provides a lot of flexibility; it combines transportation, eating facilities, and accommodation. It provides comfortable, private, and convenient commodities. Once it's outfitted, it is literally a home on wheels. Though RVs are expensive to own and operate, you save money on food and lodging, and the kids can play a game, have a nap, or make a snack with a great degree of freedom and comfort. Parents may feel a bit claustrophobic as they cook, clean, live, and drive in the same space, but if they can maneuver past that feeling *and* into a tight parking space, an RV may be a good family solution. RVs are widely available for long- or short-term leasing.

Boats or ferries are a fun way to travel. They can break up the monotony of a car ride and save time as well. Children love them, but be prepared for motion sickness (see Chapter 6), especially if the trip is lengthy.

Flying is the fastest and easiest way to travel, especially when long distances are involved. It is also usually the most expensive, and there's little sightseeing along the way (unless you count Chicago's O'Hare airport as being scenic or educational!).

Children are fascinated by trains, and love to ride on them. A train allows you the chance to look at some scenery and meet fellow travelers. Your children will have some freedom of movement, but a long trip will still be difficult for young children. As with flying, you don't have to worry about driving, road conditions, or car trouble. Train travel, however, takes more time than flying, and is not inexpensive.

■ ACCOMMODATIONS ■

You will be most comfortable in family-oriented accommodations that have the facilities and tolerance for children. Hotels with on-site restaurants and extra amenities like dry cleaning and room service are usually very clean and comfortable. Many times they are centrally located to tourist attractions. Sometimes, however, they are not convenient for families and all their gear. Hauling the kids (in my case, I feel like a parade with five kids) and tons of equipment through a hotel lobby and up the elevator can be quite a task. If you choose a hotel, try to get a quiet room away from elevators, vending machines, restaurants, and other busy areas.

Motels are usually less expensive and more convenient for families. Try to get a ground-level room where you can back the car right up to the door. Then you don't have to haul kids and luggage up and down stairs or elevators.

Check with the concierge, front desk, or reservations

manager for information on prices (are the kids free?), distance to attractions, availability of cribs, adjoining rooms, suites, laundry and kitchen facilities, parking, restaurants (is there a children's menu?), meal packages, airport or other transportation, television, recreational programs, playground equipment, tennis courts, and swimming facilities. Some hotels have nurseries or can recommend or supply sitters at an additional cost. Most hotels and motels can also provide information about special events, family attractions, and scenic or interesting aspects of the area.

Many hotels, inns, and resorts have fabulous services for kids and parents. Some offer day camps, game rooms, swimming lessons, videos, arts and crafts, playgrounds, kids' meals, and "clubs." For extended stays, these are expensive but terrific. Some hotels and resorts also offer family package plans, far below the standard rate.

Try to make your reservations as far in advance as possible, especially during peak seasons and holidays. Reservations save a lot of problems, like spending hours frantically trying to find a place to stay with a tired family in tow. If a deposit is required to hold your reservation, check on the refund policy. If you don't guarantee your reservation with a deposit or credit card, find out how late (usually between 4:00 and 6:00 P.M.) the room will be held.

Consult the list of toll-free numbers of major motel and hotel chains on pages 66-67.

■ *FINANCES* ■

There are few better ways to spend money than for the beautiful, lifelong memories and togetherness of a good family vacation. The ways to handle your trip's finances will vary depending on your personal preferences and needs. You will need to budget realistically, however. Consider the costs when deciding where to go. Obviously, some places are more expensive than others. Costs can vary considerably as you choose from camping or staying in luxury hotels, flying or touring by car, eating in nice restaurants or fixing your own food. Cut the trip down to fit your pocketbook if you need to. If you return home with money left over, use it to start next year's vacation fund.

Plan for expenses such as lodging, restaurants, activities, and transportation. It's wise to use traveler's checks since they are safer than cash, convenient, readily accepted, and can be replaced if lost or stolen.

Whenever possible, put large expenses on one major credit card. This is not only convenient but reduces the amount of money or number of traveler's checks you need to carry and helps keep track of expenditures. A credit card also provides security in case you need money for an unplanned emergency. But be careful that you don't get carried away and charge items that don't fit the budget.

You might want to save the money for your trip in a special "vacation fund" savings account. This will save you the frustration of debt, as well as money in interest charges.

Take along more money than you need. Include extra change for phone calls, tolls, pay toilets, tips, vending machines, and laundromats. Remember that unexpected expenses will come up when you're away from home, so it's not a good idea to begin on a shoestring. The wonders of the world lose a lot of their appeal if you have to count your nickels and dimes to look at them.

Money Saving Tips

Any food you bring from home or buy in a grocery store will significantly cut your expenses. Food is one of the most costly items in your vacation budget. It is especially expensive in luxury hotels, and room service is convenient but costly. Taking a picnic lunch to amusement parks can save money—their food is always expensive and sometimes not very good.

A good guidebook will give you the costs of comparable accommodations and save you money. If you're shopping for toiletries or souvenirs, stay away from hotel shops—they are usually expensive. Also, hotels commonly add surcharges to such services as long-distance telephone connections. Ask for the cost of such surcharges before you make phone calls; some hotels charge ridiculous rates for providing services you can get much less expensively from a pay phone.

Ways for Children to Handle Money

A family vacation can provide a great opportunity for discussing money matters with your kids. Teach them responsibility and the value of money by letting them earn their own spending money for the trip. A family discussion may result in a brainstorm of ideas for ways they can earn money. Older children can take care of a neighbor's pets, plants, or yard while the neighbor vacations; they can babysit, mow lawns, or shovel snow in the winter. Younger children can do extra jobs for Mom and Dad, have a toy sale or lemonade stand, or collect and recycle newspapers or aluminum cans.

You can also give each child an allowance to spend. Make sure that each child understands that when the allowance is gone, it's gone—you won't be giving out bonuses. (And don't if you ever want to be believed again!) Letting your children have some money to manage gives them some freedom to buy what they want and takes the pressure off you at every stop to "Let's get this, Mom." Decide on rules on how they can spend their money and limits on the amount to be spent.

Trip Records

Record your expenses in a trip log. It's nice to know how you spent your money, and a written record can be used for your next trip as you plan costs and budget for food, entertainment, and lodging. A look back at last year's expenditures helps you to anticipate this year's costs.

A large manila envelope can serve as the log. Note the date and location of each entry and list expenditures such as gas (include current mileage), food, lodgings, activities, gifts, and services (car repairs, laundromat, tips, etc.) on the outside. Put a pencil and any receipts, records, and other papers inside. This will consolidate your papers and keep the glove compartment from becoming a paper mess.

Souvenirs

Everything appeals to kids, no matter how ordinary or bizarre. If you want to save money and your nerves, discuss souvenir purchases with the family before you leave home. For the greatest long-lasting satisfaction, agree to get each child one special item of good quality that can really be treasured; convince the kids that a lot of worthless junk will be lost, broken, or soon forgotten. When the kids know you are buying only one gift for each child, they are more careful in their selection. My favorites are useful items like a t-shirt or hat, a well-made or educational toy, or items unique to the region. A cornhusk doll from the Blue Ridge or a beaded belt handcrafted in the Southwest has special value as a native art. If you or your child has a collection such as seashells, fossils, or even teacups or kaleidoscopes, you might want choose an addition to that collection.

> You can also compile a postcard collection of the places you visit. The children can take turns selecting a card at each major stop. For children too small to use a camera, this is a happy alternative. You can also buy a souvenir photograph book of the attraction. Children can look at the pictures and remember where they've been and what they saw.

No matter how you decide to limit your selection, still think twice when buying souvenirs. For some reason we feel we must buy "something to remember it by." Don't get so busy buying a memento that you're oblivious to the event or experience. Remember that whatever you buy, you have to get it home safely, and then tend it, clean it, and store it. Ask yourself: 1. Is it worth the money? 2. Can I get a better one at home? 3. Is it good quality? 4. Will you or the child use it? On your trip, bring home memories and less memorabilia.

■ *PREPARATION* ■

Itinerary

Make a schedule for your trip. List where you'll be, what you generally plan to see and do on each day, your route, how many miles you'll cover, where you'll stay, and what reservations are made. Estimate your mileage and expenses. You don't need to allocate every minute in an ironclad plan. Leave some flexibility so you can make needed changes.

I like to list the most appealing points of interest in each area and their cost. Then I can quickly see the options if I have more or less time. I make this easy by highlighting my guidebooks and making notes in the margins for easy reference.

> Mark your route on the map with yellow highlighter so everyone can see where you're going and in what order.

Get the whole family involved so everyone will help make easy work of the task while feeling a part of the excitement. Assign jobs, however simple, so each person is helping and sharing the experience. Don't overwork children so they feel resentful.

Try to schedule your preparations so that you can relax and get a good night's sleep the day before your trip begins. You will feel better and healthier if you aren't exhausted before you leave home.

To pique the interest of the children share your information on the places, sights, and people you will see. Read the guidebooks and brochures you've gathered in your research. Show them the road maps. They'll enjoy the trip more, and younger children won't be so surprised or frightened by new experiences.

Prepare your children by discussing the differences between home and traveling. Tell them where you're going, how long the trip will take, how far you'll go, and how much time will be spent in the car. Discuss rest stops, games, activities, treats, meals, people you'll see, and the exciting sights and activities you'll enjoy. Children will act and feel better if they understand the situation in advance. Be careful about making specific promises you might not be able to keep if your plans change.

Before you leave, discuss rules, responsibilities, and behavior so the children clearly know what is expected of them. Family rules aren't being left at home. Talk about noise, eating, finances, fighting, safety, seating arrangements, cleanup, etc. Be sure they understand how they should behave as well as how they shouldn't. This is an opportunity to clarify your expectations and point out the pitfalls that might spoil your vacation if everyone is not trying to be on best behavior.

> Teach your children good restaurant manners before you leave home. Many parents find a trip to a local eatery helpful for a pretrip practice of restaurant etiquette.

19

A day or weekend trip can be a good preparatory experience for a longer trip if the family is not used to traveling. This is an especially worthwhile exercise if you have a child who must sit in a car seat.

You can keep everyone happier and arguments to a minimum if you do what you can in your preparations to make travel comfortable and convenient. Especially if you're spending a lot of time in the car, remember to keep everything simple.

Figure out ways to save as much time on your trip as on routine tasks. Get a permanent or an easy wash-and-wear haircut so you don't have to spend time fussing with your hair. Fix your girls' hair into simple styles like pony-tails that can be done quickly and are neat as well as pretty.

If you are going to send postcards on your trip, type or write the names and addresses on self-adhesive labels before you leave home. Make sure you have stamps for letters and postcards. You don't want to spend time looking for a post office.

Before an extended trip or long-distance travel, you might want to get dental and medical checkups and copies of medication and eyeglass prescriptions. Some parents update their wills before such trips.

Before you go, leave behind some basic supplies like diapers, formula, baby food, and staples in the freezer and cupboards. Leave a clean change of clothing for each family member. Although it is not necessary, leave the house clean, if at all possible. You may be very depressed if you return to a dirty house, dirty laundry, and no food. When you're tired and facing unpacking and mountains of laundry, it's nice to come home to a clean house and be able to fix a quick meal, even if it's just macaroni or tuna sandwiches.

■ *CHECKLISTS* ■

This set of checklists will help you remember what you need to do in preparation for your trip.

Travel Arrangements

☐ Obtain maps, brochures, books, and guides

☐ Research your trip through brochures, books, maps, and talking to friends or a travel agent

☐ Make an itinerary, trip budget, and countdown schedule

☐ Make reservations for accommodations, special tours,campgrounds, transportation, and rental cars/inquire about facilities and services available and notify them of any special needs

☐ Arrange transportation to and from airport/boat/train

☐ Arrange special events: rentals, lessons, tours

☐ Tickets: Reserve, send deposits, pick up

☐ Buy travel insurance

☐ Arrange pet care with a friend or make kennel reservations; make a list of instructions

☐ Make a packing list

☐ Make up menu plans for picnics

☐ Confirm reservations and arrangements

Traveling With Children and Enjoying It

- [ ] Select clothing; pack suitcases, gear, and food
- [ ] Buy traveler's checks/get money to carry: quarters for tolls and laundry
- [ ] Give a friend or family member your traveler's checks numbers
- [ ] Leave a friend or family member your itinerary, car identification information, and name and phone numbers of where you can be reached in case of a family emergency
- [ ] Check weather report

If you are traveling abroad, add to the checklist:

- [ ] Check inoculation requirements/obtain vaccinations
- [ ] Get pictures for passport/visas
- [ ] File applications and obtain passport/visas
- [ ] Obtain international driver's license
- [ ] Buy language books and dictionaries
- [ ] Buy foreign currency

Personal Preparations

- [ ] Check the condition of luggage/buy any necessary extra pieces
- [ ] Check the condition of any equipment you're taking: skis, tennis racquets, camera, camping, water sports equipment

- [ ] Ask insurance company for procedure to follow and forms required if you need medical care

- [ ] Buy enough necessary medication to last the trip

- [ ] Obtain copies of medication and eyeglass prescriptions

- [ ] Return library books or borrowed items

- [ ] Pay bills or arrange to have bills paid while you're away

- [ ] Call broker or financial consultant to see if there are any financial decisions you need to make

- [ ] Buy any items needed for the trip: food, clothing, toiletries, equipment

- [ ] Wash, iron, dry clean, or repair clothes

- [ ] Shine or repair shoes

- [ ] Leave a clean change of clothing and basic supplies in the house for your return

- [ ] Discuss trip with children, including highlights, rules, finances, and safety

- [ ] Remove unnecessary items from wallet or purse/photocopy important contents such as credit cards, driver's license

- [ ] Prepare picnic items and food

- [ ] Make good-bye calls

Leaving Your Home

Several weeks before leaving:

☐ Arrange for a friend or neighbor to take care of your home: Bring in garbage cans, check front door for unexpected deliveries, watch the house

☐ Arrange plant care; make a list of instructions

☐ In summer, arrange for yard and garden care and watering

☐ In winter, arrange for snow to be shoveled from your driveway and sidewalks

☐ Cancel or change family commitments, lessons, or activities

☐ Purchase stamps, if you plan to send postcards

A week before leaving:

☐ In summer, set up and check automatic sprinkler system

☐ Stop newspaper delivery or ask neighbor to pick up papers

☐ Stop milk, food, or water deliveries

☐ Arrange for someone to pick up mail and parcels or have mail held at post office

☐ Notify police or security personnel, employer, landlord, child caregivers, school, household help or services, co-workers, that you will be away

☐ Move valuables out of sight to safekeeping or to a safe-deposit box

The day before leaving:

☐ Give the person watching your home instructions, extra house keys, alarm instructions and key, itinerary; car make, model, color, and license number; phone numbers where you can be reached

☐ Connect, set, and test automatic light timers and alarm system

☐ Bring in outdoor furniture and equipment

☐ Refrigerator: discard leftovers and perishable food/turn off icemaker

☐ Check pilot lights

☐ Clean house and wash dishes

☐ If not taking the car, put it in the garage or leave it with a friend or family member

When you leave:

- ☐ Turn down bell on telephone/hook up answering machine

- ☐ Turn down hot water thermostat

- ☐ Adjust heating or cooling thermostat

- ☐ Disconnect appliances from wall sockets

- ☐ Turn off faucets to washing machine and outdoor hoses

- ☐ Close fireplace flues

- ☐ Take out garbage

- ☐ Run garbage disposal

- ☐ Make sure toilets are flushed and not running

- ☐ Secure and lock windows

- ☐ Lock all doors

Getting the Car Ready

Before you leave:

- ☐ Buy insurance for travel and towing

- ☐ Have the car serviced: oil change, tune-up, lube job

- [ ] Check the air conditioning, battery, brakes, steering, clutch/transmission, muffler, exhaust system, hoses, fan belts, wiring, signals, lights, filters, wiper blades, alignment, seat belts

- [ ] Check fluid levels: battery, radiator, oil, windshield-washer fluid tank

- [ ] Buy spare fuses, fan belts, hoses, wiper blades, and special fluids that you might need

- [ ] Empty glove compartment of unnecessary items

- [ ] Put important papers and small items in glove compartment

- [ ] Empty trunk of unnecessary items

- [ ] Make sure the car equipment is packed (see list on pages 28-31)

- [ ] Hook up trailers and hitches/Check electrical connections on directional signals

- [ ] Put on special racks: luggage, ski, bike

- [ ] Wash car and windows/Clean interior

- [ ] Put in a clean trash bag

- [ ] Pack car and trunk

- [ ] Fill up with gas or diesel fuel

- [ ] Check tires and tire pressure, including the spare tire

Car Equipment

A sports bag with a shoulder strap can be stored in the trunk to keep these items together, clean, and easy to find. In case of an emergency this bag can be easily taken along if you need to leave the car. I live in earthquake country so there's a lot of security knowing it's there. Accident or a natural disaster may warrant the extra precaution of including snacks, water, and a few survival items in a car equipment list.

- [ ] Spare tire (inflated and in good repair)
- [ ] Jack/lug wrench/wedges
- [ ] Air pump/aerosol tire inflater
- [ ] Tire pressure gauge
- [ ] Flares/reflectors
- [ ] Emergency flag/windshield "help/call police" sign
- [ ] Jumper cables
- [ ] Tow chain
- [ ] Spare parts: fan belts, wiper blades, fuses, special fluids, hoses
- [ ] Flashlight/extra batteries
- [ ] Gas can
- [ ] Can of motor oil/spout/can opener
- [ ] Rope/wire/electrical tape

- [ ] Tool kit: pliers, Phillips and regular screwdrivers, crescent wrench, socket set
- [ ] Folding shovel
- [ ] Pocketknife
- [ ] Compass
- [ ] Magnetic key box with extra keys
- [ ] Fire extinguisher
- [ ] Emergency space blanket
- [ ] Ground cloth/plastic (to use while working on car)
- [ ] Jumpsuit/old shirt and shoes (to wear while working on car)
- [ ] Work gloves
- [ ] Rags
- [ ] Jug of drinking water
- [ ] Collapsible cup
- [ ] Suction-cup car sun shade
- [ ] First aid kit/book
- [ ] Medications: basic, prescribed, motion sickness (pack medicine so children can't get into it)
- [ ] Plastic bags for trash or motion sickness

☐ Whisk broom

☐ Glass cleaner/paper towels/sponge

☐ Comfort items: seat cushion/air freshener/cup holder

☐ Winter: ice scraper and brush/chains/snow tires/sand/rock salt/de-icer

Important Papers

☐ Registration

☐ Driver's license

☐ Insurance telephone number/identification card

☐ Auto club/towing cards

☐ Gasoline credit cards

☐ Car repair manual/instruction booklet/list of dealers and service center

☐ Maps

Personal Items

☐ Driving gloves

☐ Eyeglasses/sunglasses

☐ Spare change

☐ Comb

- ☐ Pen/pencil/paper/envelopes
- ☐ Tissues/napkins/towelettes/wet wipes
- ☐ Extra diaper/tampon
- ☐ Car games/activities
- ☐ Snacks (nonperishable)
- ☐ Can opener/matches
- ☐ Radio/tape player/cassettes/earphones
- ☐ Blanket/pillow
- ☐ Umbrella/rain gear
- ☐ Reading matter
- ☐ A copy of *Traveling With Children and Enjoying It*

CHAPTER 2

What To Take

What to Take

Deciding what to take on your vacation can be difficult, but getting it to fit into the space available is even harder. You want enough for your needs (or is that need enough for your wants?), but you don't want to be bogged down with too much. You know you're supposed to travel light, but the memory of the aggravation you felt the last time you forgot some necessary item still irritates you. This chapter will give you some packing tips and ideas on how to get organized. It includes checklists you can use to make the whole process as simple and easy as possible.

■ WARDROBE PLANNING ■

By planning your wardrobe you can have the right amount of clothing that is most suitable for the circumstances. When choosing your wardrobe, consider how much you want to carry. This is affected by how often you pack and unpack and your mode of transportation. Consider your destination—are you going to a city or a resort? Will you be at the beach or in a campground? Choose clothes best suited to your activities. Plan clothes appropriate for sports, formal affairs, picnicking, or sightseeing. Of course, you will have to consider the season and weather. Finally, consider whether you will be willing or able to do laundry.

You can stretch your travel wardrobe and avoid overpacking by following a few guidelines. These following tips are directed to the whole family, but with a focus on adults. Tips especially for children can be found later in the chapter.

Take clothes that fit well, are clean and comfortable, and are in good repair. Choose fabrics that are easy to care for. They should be washable, wrinkle-resistant, and quick to dry. First, color-coordinate your choices. Choose separates in several basic colors and add a few bright colored pieces for accent. You can mix and match items to create different looks.

Second, select simple clothing that will serve multiple purposes. A crisp pair of cotton slacks, for instance, can be dressed up or toned down with a change of belt or sash. Jewelry, scarves, and belts take up little space but can change a basic daytime look to an elegant evening one. As you choose accent pieces, consider temperature changes and layer your outfit accordingly.

Accessories should be simple and versatile. Women should bring one handbag that is neutral in both style and color. It will go with everything. Choose one with a shoulder strap to help keep your hands free. A neutral sweater and a lightweight but warm coat for each person should adapt to most weather conditions.

If you are truly committed to traveling light, you really need only two pairs of comfortable shoes per person. Choose one for casual and the other for dress. You might also want slip-on sandals or thongs that can double for slippers. Rubber thongs are great at the beach, in public showers, or even in a warm rain. Women should choose a nightgown that can double as a robe.

■ PACKING GUIDELINES AND TIPS ■

Many of us pack with the assumptions that we won't select the right items, we will forget something we need, we won't have enough clothes, or we will be caught off guard by an unexpected event. These fears are usually unfounded, and besides, this book is designed to help you stay on track. Just remember, if you overpack there's more to forget, lose, take care of, and worry about. If you pack only what you need you'll be able to find your clothes faster and you'll have less to haul around. Excess baggage is cumbersome, time consuming, and expensive if you're charged for storage. Don't try to take everything!

I like what Marty Leshner says about packing:

"Into a case designed to hold two suits, many of us attempt to stuff the contents of an entire walk-in closet. Predictably, these `carefully selected' clothes fall into distinct categories: those we cannot live without, those we have never worn in our lives but will finally use on this trip, and those that will look good once we get a tan. Place all of these wardrobe 'essentials' on your bed and mercilessly cut back."*

These guidelines and ideas will help you be ruthless and get the job done. Begin by tagging all your luggage on the inside with your name, address, and phone number; tag on the outside with your name, business and/or destination address, and your home phone number. For air travel, see Chapter 4 for more ideas. Start to pack early to avoid stress and last-minute rush. (Anything you can keep permanently packed, to be used only on trips, will save time, work, and worry. I do this with a diaper bag, a toiletry bag, a first aid kit, a picnic box, and cooking supplies.) It is important *where* you pack things. What good is it if you can't find or get to it?

---

* Copyright 1987 Automobile Club of Southern California, reproduction by permission, courtesy of WESTWAYS and M. Leshner

Leave behind valuable jewelry or special or sentimental items. You will eliminate worry about their loss or theft. Discourage children from taking along special items; explain how easily belongings can be left behind when traveling and how difficult retrieval may be. If a child simply cannot sleep without a special object, limit its use to car or lodging; don't bring it to parks, museums, or restaurants.

If you plan to use your best clothes only once or twice, pack everyone's together in a separate suitcase. This case can then be grabbed when it's needed. Most importantly, the clothes stay neat and clean. Plastic hangers can be used to hang clothes in a bathroom to "steam out" wrinkles. Similarly, keep your coats in a separate bag. When you need coats usually everyone does, and you won't have to dig through suitcases to find them.

On long trips take enough clothing for one week and do a weekly laundry. Put dirty clothing in a large heavy-duty trash bag so you have dirty laundry in one place. You can grab the bag easily if you go to a laundromat. You can also take a bag in the car with an emergency change of clothing for everyone. Then, if someone becomes messy or clean clothes run out unexpectedly, you don't have to run to the laundromat or return to your lodgings to clean up.

When you pack prescription medications, leave them in their original containers so they're not confiscated as illegal drugs. Put the bottles in a plastic, resealable zip-type bag so you don't have to worry about leakage. Stock up on sundries such as film, toothpaste, shampoo, cosmetics, and medications. They may be difficult to find on your travels and may be expensive.

To save room, leave novels at home and read disposable materials such as brochures, catalogs, newspapers, and magazines. If possible, shop for your souvenirs and gifts on the last day of the trip, so that you don't have to pack them around or worry about loss or breakage. Carry them in an expandable bag, a small fold-up tote bag, or a duffel bag that won't take up much room.

Lastly, if you are going to a foreign country, check to see if you need a voltage converter and set of plugs for your electrical appliances (hair dryers, electric shavers, etc.). Bring them along even if your reservations are made in hotels which have assured you that converters aren't necessary. You never know how your plans might change.

■ *PACKING FOR CHILDREN* ■

It's hard to keep from overpacking children's gear, but it can be done. Cut down on baby gear as much as possible by renting, borrowing, improvising, or doing without. You will be surprised at what you can devise. An umbrella stroller is wonderful to take because it is lightweight, easy to use, and folds to a compact size. It offers you a chance to relieve your arms (even infants can be heavy after a while) and the child a comfortable place to rest or sleep. It also doubles as a highchair. A collapsible playpen can double as a crib, and a car seat can also be an infant carrier. Many parents of infants and toddlers find soft fabric infant carriers or lightweight frame carriers to be indispensable; if, however, you find these are uncomfortable on your back or shoulders, leave them at home. Backpacks make wonderful diaper bags; they can easily be attached to strollers and leave your hands free.

As for clothing, the bad news is that children will need more changes of clothing than adults, but the good news is that their clothes take less space. Make sure the clothes fit if they are new or haven't been worn recently. Leave home clothes they dislike. Let the kids help choose the selection and be sure to include at least some favorite items. Play clothes offer comfort, durability, and peace of mind for parents; save dress-up clothes for specific events. Similarly, stretch suits are nice for baby because they're so versatile: they're compact, they protect the child well against sun, cold, or insects, and they alleviate the need for booties.

Jogging suits are comfortable and can double as pajamas. Don't take children's robes; they take up too much room. An older child who feels the need to be modest can select a sweatsuit or nightgown that can do double-duty as a robe.

Shoes should be broken in, comfortable for walking, and easy to put on. If you have kids who won't keep their shoes on, take sandals or thongs in the car that can be put on quickly for short stops. As mentioned previously, thongs are also good for the beach, pool, public showers, or to use as slippers.

Baby clothes should be packed in one separate, accessible suitcase; you will be needing it often. Small clothing gets lost easily when packed with larger clothing, and you can see what's still available for use. (Have you ever searched three suitcases looking for a pair of baby socks?) You might want to include an extra pacifier in case one gets lost or misplaced. Consider bringing a small blanket that can be used as a comforter, a changing pad, a sleeping mat, or a stroller or car seat cover. It can also provide privacy for nursing and can be used to create a play or picnicking area.

Take a few familiar, favorite items such as a doll, stuffed animal, or blanket that will provide comfort in strange surroundings. If your child always carries around a favorite toy, this is not the time to break the dependency. As mentioned before, however, these items are often easy to lose and difficult to find, so you may have to put limits on where it can be loved. If you are visiting other children, put an identifying mark or the children's names on their toys.

If you are not traveling by car and food and diapers will be readily available, it's easier to buy them as you go or upon arrival rather than packing and carrying around a two-week supply. Don't let your supply get so low that you're caught frantically searching for a store. Put a roll of Lifesavers®, granola bars, or small boxes of raisins in your purse for emergencies.

■ PACKING THE SUITCASES ■

Successful packing depends on two efforts on your part: to conserve space and to be organized. Experiment with different packing strategies. You can pack one suitcase for each person; you can have a number of people share a suitcase, or you can put all the family's clothing for one day in one suitcase so that only one case is used each day. Whichever way you prefer, begin by choosing a suitcase neither too large nor too small for the amount you are taking. Pack items in the order you'll use them. In other words, pack first what you'll use last.

To conserve space, roll your clothes, smoothing them as you go. If you prefer to fold some times, at least roll underwear and pajamas to fill in the small empty spaces. To help keep clothes from wrinkling, pack the bag tightly so clothing can't slide around easily. Rolled clothing will usually have fewer wrinkles, but if you fold certain pieces, use as few folds as possible, keeping natural creases in mind. Tie your clothing in place with suitcase ties and use tissue paper or plastic bags around clothing folds and in empty spaces.

To pack shoes put the shoe insides together with heels at opposite ends. Then place shoes inside plastic bags to keep the clothing clean. Put small items like socks and underwear inside shoes to use up otherwise wasted space.

Pack heavy objects like a hair dryer or shoes close to the hinges of your suitcase. When the suitcase is closed and upright, they will be at the bottom and won't slide down and wrinkle your clothing. Cushion fragile items like a travel alarm, electric shaver, or toiletry bag with soft articles of clothing. Diapers do a great job as cushions and, if you use them to fill corners as well, you may not have to make room for a large box of them.

For children, roll each day's outfit together. You can wrap an elastic band around each bundle or put them in regular plastic bags with a twist tie or resealable zip-type plastic bags. Mark the child's name on the bag. Each day each child can easily take a bundle without searching through the suitcase, making a mess or ending up with mismatched clothes. When you get home you can see what's not been worn so you don't have to wash everything.

For older children, tape packing lists to the lids of their suitcases and let them do their own packing. Have them check off each item as it is packed.

■ PACKING THE CAR ■

Pack the car the night before you leave if you can put your car in a locked garage or if you live in a safe area. This will give you a chance to make sure everything fits before the

last minute. It will also save a lot of time when you're in a hurry to leave.

> Don't pack the car with the kids around if at all possible. You can work faster and more effectively by yourself. Children have a tendency to "mysteriously" add items they "need."

Pack the car so the family has as much room as possible in the car to stretch, sleep, or play. An overcrowded car is confining and uncomfortable. To make more room inside the car, put the luggage in the trunk or use a rooftop luggage rack or carrier. Distribute weight evenly so the car isn't hard to handle.

If you are taking sports equipment like bicycles or skis, ask your car dealer or sporting goods store manager if special carriers are available to help transport them.

As you pack, organize the car so items you will need along the way are easy to reach. This is especially true of the front-seat tote, coats, blankets, water, snacks, and baby food, clothes, and diapers. If you are using a sedan, don't pack anything on the rear window ledge. Loose bags can fall forward and injure passengers, and they often block the driver's vision of the road.

■ *MORE PACKING IDEAS* ■

Plastic Bags: Plastic bags with twist ties, resealable zip-type plastic bags, and plastic grocery bags with handles have

many uses for family trips. They hold picnics, trash, kids' treasured collections, wet clothing, bathing suits, or any items that can leak. They're handy for emergencies like motion sickness and they can be used to wrap up any item that you would like to keep clean. Large trash bags are handy for coats or other clothing as well as dirty laundry. They can be used as a mattress cover if you have a bed wetter or as a clean, nonporous layer between you and a dirty or wet surface. They can be stuffed in odd places but can tear easily.

Tote or Duffel Bags: These versatile bags can be stuffed with blankets, coats, regular clothing, an emergency change of clothing, dirty laundry, sports equipment, toys, and more. They can be packed and grabbed easily; they can double as pillows; and they will store items away from dirt.

Front-Seat Tote Bag: I like to keep a large tote bag in the front seat of the car so items I use regularly are readily accessible. My bag usually includes maps, guidebooks, camera, binoculars, motion sickness medicine, routine medications, sunglasses, wet wipes, a trash bag, plastic bags, paper cups, paper towels (for spills), snacks or treats, disposable diapers, a pencil and note pad (for games), a journal, needlework, and a book or magazine for me (I've never been able to read yet, but one can always hope!). In case a restroom is lacking basic needs, I also take soap in a plastic case, paper toilet seat covers, and tissues.

Pajama Bag: You can pack all the nightwear for the family together since it's used at the same time. If you're tired, you can bring in just this one bag, and everyone can get ready for bed without delay. This works well with the one-suitcase-a-day packing method. You can bring the next day's clothes in with you or get them in the morning.

Swimwear Bag: Pack everyone's swimwear together in a special bag. When you decide to go swimming, you only have to find and sort through one bag, and everyone is ready to go. Include swimsuits, caps, towels, cover-ups, water toys, sunglasses, lotions, nose and ear plugs, a comb, and a plastic bag for wet items.

■ USING A CHECKLIST ■

You can pack quickly and with confidence if you use packing lists each time. Tape them to the lids of your suitcases so that they're handy to check to make sure you don't forget an important item. Save your packing lists from trip to trip. They help you remember good ideas from previous trips and are a starting point for the next trip. Remember to write down additions to the list as you think of them.

Make a list of items that can't be packed until the last minute and put it in a conspicuous place. Try to cut this list as much as possible. This is easily done with inexpensive, replaceable items. For example, you can buy a set of travel toothbrushes that stay in your toiletries bag, but a favorite bedtime stuffed toy will have to be added last.

I have included several checklists for you to use. To personalize these lists, put a check next to every item you take. When you get home, add any items that you want to take next time, and cross off what you didn't need.

Essential Items

- ☐ wallet/purse

- ☐ money/traveler's checks/credit cards/checkbook

- ☐ identification/driver's licenses for all drivers

- ☐ car and house keys/duplicate set

- ☐ eyeglasses/contact lenses/lens cleaner

- ☐ watch

- ☐ medical papers: insurance cards and forms/medical alert cards/extra copy of medical and eyeglass prescriptions

☐ travel papers: itinerary, tickets, reservation confirmations and receipts, vouchers, directions, packing lists, traveler's checks serial numbers

☐ maps/guidebooks/brochures

☐ phone numbers: medical, insurance, friends and family, bank, credit cards (if lost or stolen)

Accessories

☐ diary/ledger

☐ date book/address book

☐ writing supplies: pens, pencil, paper, postcards, envelopes, stamps

☐ briefcase/tote/backpack

☐ camera/film/flash/film mailers

☐ books/magazines/newspapers

☐ toys/cards/games

☐ radio/tape player/tapes/earphones

☐ flashlight/extra batteries

☐ umbrella/rain gear

☐ laundry items: bag, hangers, clothes pins, detergent, softener, spot remover, quarters for machines

☐ plastic bags/twist ties

☐ towels/washcloth/disposable cloth wipes

☐ travel iron

☐ pocketknife

☐ jewelry

☐ sunglasses

☐ travel alarm clock

☐ sewing kit: needle/thread/scissors/safety pins

☐ first aid kit/book

☐ blankets/pillows

Basic Eating Supplies

☐ food/snacks/candy/gum

☐ water/beverages/jug/canteen

☐ cooler/ice

☐ paper cups/collapsible cups

☐ paper napkins/paper towels/wet wipes

☐ can and bottle opener/knife

Special Equipment

☐ sports equipment: Frisbee, fishing gear, kite, ball, tennis racquets and balls, bicycles, water equipment, skis

☐ binoculars

☐ hobby items/musical instruments

☐ pet equipment/supplies

Toiletries Bag

Keep a toiletry bag permanently packed so you don't have to reassemble these needs each time. I use one bag for the boys in the family, and one for the girls. Use sample sizes of toothpaste, lotion, and shampoo. Put lotions, shampoos, aspirin, and jewelry into small medicine containers or 35mm film cases; plastic containers are also sold in drug stores. Label each container. Small objects or supplies that might leak can be packed into zip-type plastic bags. Instead of taking bottles that can break or leak, moisten cotton balls with liquids like perfumes and fingernail polish remover and place them in a container.

☐ toothbrushes/toothpaste/dental floss

☐ breath freshener/mouthwash

☐ deodorant

☐ combs/brushes

- ☐ shampoo/conditioner/shower cap
- ☐ curling iron/hair dryer/curlers
- ☐ hair styling items: barrettes/ribbons/elastics
- ☐ mirror
- ☐ hand soap/dish soap (to wash baby bottles, etc.)
- ☐ perfume/cologne
- ☐ skin care lotions/sunscreen lotions/lip balm
- ☐ insect repellent
- ☐ shaving gear: razor and blades, cream, aftershave lotion, electric razor
- ☐ cosmetics: foundation, powder, blush, lipstick, eye makeup, makeup remover
- ☐ nail care equipment/tweezers/scissors
- ☐ tissues/towelettes/cotton balls/swabs
- ☐ feminine hygiene items
- ☐ medications

Women's Clothing

- ☐ underpants/bra/slip
- ☐ socks/panty hose

- ☐ dresses/skirts
- ☐ blouses: casual/dress
- ☐ pants: casual/jeans/dress
- ☐ shorts
- ☐ sportswear
- ☐ evening wear: gowns/purse/shoes
- ☐ belts/scarves/handkerchiefs
- ☐ nightgown/robe/slippers
- ☐ shoes: casual/dress/sandals/athletic
- ☐ swimwear: bathing suit/cap/cover-up
- ☐ coat/jacket/sweater
- ☐ winterwear: gloves/boots/hat

Men's Clothing

- ☐ underpants/T-shirts
- ☐ socks: sport/dress
- ☐ shirts: sport/dress
- ☐ pants: jeans/casual/dress
- ☐ shorts

☐ sportswear

☐ suit/sports jacket

☐ ties/tie pin/cuff links

☐ belts/handkerchiefs

☐ pajamas/robe/slippers

☐ shoes: dress/casual/athletic

☐ swimwear: bathing suit

☐ coat/jacket/sweater

☐ winterwear: gloves/boots/hat

Children's Clothing

☐ underpants/T-shirts

☐ socks

☐ play clothes: shirts/ shorts, pants, or jeans/sweat-suits/summer outfits

☐ dress clothes

☐ accessories: belt, hair care items

☐ pajamas

☐ shoes: dress/play/thongs

☐ swimsuits

☐ coat/jacket/sweater

☐ winter outerwear: gloves/boots/hat

Baby Clothing

☐ disposable diapers/diapers/diaper covers

☐ undershirts

☐ stretch suits/sleepers

☐ day outfits

☐ dress clothes

☐ booties/socks

☐ shoes

☐ sweater/jacket/coat/snowsuit/bunting

Baby Equipment

☐ diaper bag (see next list)

☐ umbrella stroller

☐ car seat/booster seat

☐ backpack child carrier/front carrier

☐ child wrist hand holder

☐ portable crib/playpen

- ☐ sheets (crib and waterproof)/blankets

- ☐ portable tabletop high chair

- ☐ potty seat

- ☐ bottle-warming equipment

- ☐ medications/vitamins/thermometer

- ☐ night light

- ☐ bathing supplies: towel, washcloth, soap, shampoo, powder, lotions/creams

- ☐ nail clippers

- ☐ toys/stuffed animal/books

Diaper Bag

Keep a diaper bag in the car stocked and ready to go for short day trips. That way you're always prepared. When you get home, restock it for the next time. Add extra supplies for longer trips. Make sure it has a shoulder strap for easy carrying.

- ☐ disposable diapers

- ☐ changing pad

- ☐ zip-type plastic bags

- ☐ wet wipes/tissues

☐ powder/lotions

☐ nursing pads/burp pad/bib

☐ baby food/plastic spoon

☐ small plastic bowl with lid

☐ bottles/nipples/caps

☐ formula/ready-to-feed bottle of juice/nipple set

☐ training cup

☐ pacifier

☐ change of clothing

☐ jacket/sweater

☐ small blanket

☐ toys

Trip Abroad

Use the regular packing lists, but add the following:

☐ passports/visas

☐ vaccination/inoculation certificates

☐ international driver's license

☐ foreign currency/currency converter

☐ foreign-language books

☐ electricity converter or adapter/plugs

☐ translated medical alert and medical insurance cards

☐ addresses and telephone numbers of embassies, consulates

Flight Carry-on Bag

Depending on your circumstances, choose from among these items:

☐ wallet/money/credit cards/traveler's checks/checkbook

☐ passport/visas

☐ identification

☐ driver's licenses

☐ travel papers: tickets, vouchers, reservation confirmations and receipts, itinerary, directions, maps, traveler's checks serial numbers

☐ keys

☐ jewelry

☐ valuables/breakables

☐ eyeglasses/contact lenses/sunglasses

☐ medical alert card/insurance identification card

- ☐ medications
- ☐ camera/film/flash
- ☐ books/magazines/guidebooks
- ☐ toys/cards/games
- ☐ pens/paper/writing supplies
- ☐ gum/snacks/candy
- ☐ sweater/coat/jacket/umbrella
- ☐ change of clothing
- ☐ comb/brush
- ☐ toothbrush/toothpaste
- ☐ shaving gear/cosmetics/toiletries
- ☐ tissues/towelettes
- ☐ baby supplies: diapers, bib, food, formula, bottles, blanket, pacifier

Mini Desk

A compact mini desk with a collection of writing supplies can be handy if you have correspondence or paperwork to do. Older children will also enjoy these kits. Zippered cases that hold basic desk items can be purchased in stationery or gift stores, or you can assemble your own kit in a small box, tackle box, or briefcase.

- [ ] tape/glue stick
- [ ] blunt scissors
- [ ] stapler/paper clips
- [ ] ruler
- [ ] pen/pencil
- [ ] paper/stationery/note pad
- [ ] envelopes/postcards/stamps
- [ ] date book/address book
- [ ] paperwork/correspondence
- [ ] pocket calculator
- [ ] tape recorder/blank tape

Beach Bag

- [ ] towels
- [ ] blanket
- [ ] beach chairs
- [ ] umbrella
- [ ] picnic basket/food
- [ ] cooler/ice

- [ ] water/beverages/thermos/jug

- [ ] paper and plastic tableware: cups, plates, utensils, napkins, food containers

- [ ] trash bags

- [ ] water play equipment/air pump

- [ ] sand toys: Frisbee/ball/kite

- [ ] book/magazine

- [ ] pen/pencil/paper/writing supplies

- [ ] radio/tape player/tapes/earphones

- [ ] wallet/money/identification

- [ ] keys/watch

- [ ] tanning creams/sunscreen/lip balm

- [ ] insect repellent

- [ ] comb/brush/hair care supplies

- [ ] sunglasses

- [ ] sun visor/hat

- [ ] swimsuits

- [ ] robe/cover-up

- [ ] sandals/thongs

- ☐ change of clothing
- ☐ plastic bag for wet clothes

Picnic Supplies

Keep a box packed and ready to go with basic nonperishable supplies.

- ☐ picnic basket/food
- ☐ cooler/ice
- ☐ water/beverages
- ☐ thermos/jug/canteen
- ☐ plastic tablecloth
- ☐ paper and plastic tableware: cups, plates, bowls, utensils, napkins
- ☐ serving spoons/knives/can and bottle opener
- ☐ food containers/bowls/lids
- ☐ aluminum foil/plastic wrap
- ☐ hand soap
- ☐ plastic bags: trash, twist ties, resealable zip-type
- ☐ disposable cloth wipes/paper towels/wet wipes
- ☐ apron/bib

- [ ] catsup/mustard/condiments/salt and pepper/sugar
- [ ] masking tape/elastic bands
- [ ] blanket
- [ ] sports equipment: Frisbee, ball, kite, fishing gear and license
- [ ] insect repellent
- [ ] flashlight/extra batteries
- [ ] radio/tape recorder/tapes/earphones
- [ ] camera/film
- [ ] personal gear: sunglasses, sun lotions, hat, rain gear, sweater, jacket
- [ ] toys/games/cards/book/magazine

Cooking Equipment

- [ ] matches/lighter
- [ ] pancake turner/meat fork/tongs
- [ ] frying pan/griddle/dutch oven
- [ ] saucepan/kettle with lids
- [ ] pot holder/mitt
- [ ] dishtowel/dishcloth/detergent/scouring pad/dishpan

- ☐ firewood
- ☐ charcoal
- ☐ lighter fluid/fire starters/newspaper
- ☐ grill/portable barbecue/camp stove/fuel

Additional Cooking Equipment for Camping

- ☐ long-handled utensils/skewers/roasting sticks
- ☐ cutting board/wooden spoon/whisk
- ☐ vegetable peeler/grater/egg holder
- ☐ measuring cups and spoons
- ☐ dishpan
- ☐ outdoor cookbook

Camping Equipment

As with all the lists, you'll need to take what fits your needs and activities. To make this list complete, add the picnic box items and cooking equipment.

- ☐ tent/poles/stakes
- ☐ tarp/ground cloths/mat
- ☐ sleeping bags

- ☐ air mattresses/cots/foam pads
- ☐ dining canopy/screen house
- ☐ folding chairs/campstools
- ☐ folding table
- ☐ blankets/pillows
- ☐ towels/washcloths
- ☐ air pump/inflater
- ☐ heater/camp fuel/propane canisters
- ☐ lantern/fuel
- ☐ portable lamp/flashlights/extra batteries
- ☐ patch kit: tent, raft, air mattresses, bicycle
- ☐ tools: saw, hatchet, ax, folding shovel, hammer and nails
- ☐ rope/string
- ☐ clothesline/clothespins
- ☐ whisk broom/dustpan
- ☐ portable toilet/toilet paper/plastic bags/chemical deodorant/disinfectant
- ☐ backpack

- ☐ binoculars/compass/whistle
- ☐ pocketknife/buck knife
- ☐ heavy gloves
- ☐ songbook/musical instrument
- ☐ first aid kit and book/snake bite kit

CHAPTER 3

On the Road

On the Road

You've planned and packed, and now everyone is ready to go. Review your lists, check the lights and locks, take the kids to the potty, and you will be on to the next phase: getting there.

■ *ACCOMMODATIONS* ■

Ideally you should make reservations before you leave home, but sometimes you will travel shorter or longer distances than you've planned. If you don't have reservations, stop early so you can find a place to stay while there are still vacancies and before everyone is tired and hungry. It's a good idea to have directories of possible places to stay. Motel chains often provide nationwide guides with the phone numbers, costs, amenities, and locations of their facilities. Regional travel guides often list partial information on accommodations, as do brochures from state tourism departments. Other sources are Mobil Travel Guides, *Trailer Life Campground and RV Services Directory, Rand McNally Campground Guide,* and AAA (American Automobile Association) Tourbooks.

The national hotel and motel chains provide toll-free telephone numbers for reservations and current information on their accommodations.

Best Western (800) 528-1234
Budget Host Inns (800) 283-4678
Clarion/Comfort/Quality Inns (800) 221-2222

Days Inn (800) 325-2525
Econo Lodge (800) 446-6900
Hampton Inns (800) 426-7866
Hilton Hotels (800) 345-6565
Holiday Inns (800) Holiday
Howard Johnson Hotels (800) 654-2000
Hyatt Hotels (800) 233-1234
LaQuinta (800) 531-5900
Marriott Hotels (800) 228-9290
Radisson Hotels (800) 333-3333
Ramada Inns (800) 228-2828
Sheraton (800) 325-3535
Super 8 Motels (800) 843-1991
Travelodge (800) 255-3050

At your lodgings give the children a spot to put their toys and bags. Designate a large trash bag for dirty clothes and a spot for shoes to help prevent shoe searches. For comfort, keep everything as organized and cleaned up as you can. If you need to, move the furniture to suit your purposes.

Check the room for safety. Keep the doors locked, and don't open them unless you know your visitor. Never leave a child alone in a motel.

To entertain children in a motel, let them play with toys and card games from home, watch television, make and fly paper airplanes, or play party games. Simon Says, Wastebasket Toss (see who can toss the most wads of paper into a wastebasket set at a specific distance from the toss line), or Hot and Cold (hide an object and help players locate it by saying cold, cool, warm, warmer, hot, and red hot as they move closer to it) are good for indoor play.

Get your kids out for some exercise whenever you can. Swim in the motel or hotel pool, go to a park, or take a walk. Many resorts as well as many inns have bicycles you can borrow or rent for local riding. Some bicycle rental shops have bicycle "surreys" that the whole family can pedal and ride.

Make sure you have the address and telephone number of the hotel or motel in case you leave something behind. If you don't have the information written in a logbook, take a business card, grab a matchbook, or a piece of stationery with the information you need. Most hotel or motel bills will include an address and telephone number.

■ *STAYING WITH FRIENDS & RELATIVES* ■

When you stay with friends and relatives, be considerate of their home. Keep your belongings together in one separate area. This strategy will keep you organized and help prevent lost or forgotten items. Most importantly, it will keep your disruption of your hosts' home to a minimum.

Prepare toys and activities to entertain your children and make efforts to keep them out of trouble. If you have a small child, ask if you can do some childproofing. Watch your children at all times—don't assume that others are watching or that the kids will be all right unsupervised.

Learn and keep your hosts' house rules. Ask about anything you're not sure of rather than guess wrong and create bad feelings. Discuss accommodations ahead of time and coordinate schedules so that no one is surprised or inconvenienced. Let your hosts know any specific needs you might have. Suggestions of foods the kids would enjoy will probably be appreciated if you are asked.

Be sensitive to your hosts' moods and feelings. It can be tiring to have houseguests. Don't expect your hosts to plan everything, go everywhere, or to entertain you nonstop. They might get tired of sightseeing or need some time to themselves.

> To let your hosts know you appreciate their hospitality, bring a thank-you gift, take them out to dinner, provide some groceries, help clean up the house, or include their children on one of your outings so they can have time alone. Be sure to send a thank-you note when you return home.

■ *DRIVING SCHEDULE* ■

It seems to work out best to get a good night's sleep, arise early, and get on the road as soon as possible. Some parents put their children back to sleep in the car, stopping later at a park to eat breakfast and run off some energy.

If you have a long stretch of road to cover, you can put the kids to sleep and travel part of the night. Driving a long distance is easier without restless children, and they won't notice the miles going by while they're asleep. Remember to get gas before the kids fall asleep since stopping usually wakes them up. Don't drive when you are too tired, and be careful not to get your own inner clock so turned around that you're ready to go to bed just as the kids are getting up.

Driving can also be scheduled during your children's regular naptime. You can't do much else during their nap, unless you're willing to forgo the nap and have cross children.

If you get up early on your trip you'll have more daylight hours available for sightseeing. Many attractions open early and sights of natural beauty are often breathtaking in the early morning hours. Late starts often prove frustrating—you may not have the time to do and see all that you planned. Many points of interest close at five o'clock or at sunset. You may find yourself with a carload of wideawake kids with no place to go.

Whenever possible, travel on weekdays when traffic is lighter. One of the only advantages to weekend travel is that road repair work usually ceases. Avoid driving around a large city during peak commuting hours, usually 7:00-9:00 A.M. and 4:00-6:00 P.M. If you have the time to spare, choose a scenic drive that's pretty and interesting; save the interstate highways for days when you need to cover distances quickly.

When you stop early you can more easily find a place to stay, have a leisurely supper, unwind, and have time to play, swim, and explore the area where you're staying. Everyone looks forward to the slower activities of a pleasant evening.

Change your plans if a child gets overtired or ill. If you find you're not enjoying yourself, plan another activity that sounds interesting. Some of your best experiences can come from unplanned side trips or unexpected area events or sights. Try to have a balance between time in the car, rest stops, exercise, and sleep. Everyone will feel better. Don't put yourself on a strict driving schedule where you have to cover so many miles per day or between meals. You'll just make everyone tired, miserable, and grouchy. It's not a safe situation, either. Of course, on some days you'll need to cover a certain distance, but try to alternate long and short driving days so the family doesn't get too weary and the trip doesn't become an endurance test. A good rule of thumb is to drive no more than 300 miles per day.

Know your family's limit. Remember that a long drive is hard on a child. Children can't sit still for a long time. A family with older children will be able to handle more driving than a family with younger children. Drivers have limits, too. You'll need to change drivers regularly for safety and to avoid tiring one person. Changing drivers about once every 100 miles usually works out the best.

To help the family get the most from your new experiences, discuss each day what you'll see and do. Explain what's expected of them. Announce any special events or treats early so everyone can look forward to them.

Tell children they are going to have a great time and remind them again when they're having it! This might sound unnecessary, but try it and you will see the difference.

■ REST STOPS ■

Remember that children become bored more easily than adults. Stopping will relieve the tedium of driving and may also provide an interesting, educational experience. A change will energize bored travelers and keep them interested and excited about the trip. A respite from the monotony of driving will make traveling more comfortable and more enjoyable for the whole family. The driver can use the opportunity to check the car, consult maps, get gas, or even take a short nap.

Don't wait to stop until everyone is stiff, cranky, and miserable. A stop about every two hours seems to work best, but each family and driver will have their own driving tolerance and stopping needs. Rest stops don't need to be long. Just leave the car for a few minutes, change drivers, let the kids run off some energy, and use the restroom.

Before you stop, give the kids a warning so they can get ready. Remind them to comb hair, put on shoes and coats, and clean up toys. Then when you stop everyone's ready to go instead of searching for shoes and tripping over belongings.

Get babies or toddlers out of their car seats also. Infants also need fresh air and the chance to exercise or stretch.

Use your rest stops to add to the adventure and enjoyment. Stop along the way to read historical markers, see a view, take some pictures, visit a museum, look at a gift shop, have a treat, take a walk, and explore tourist attractions and towns. Try to plan stops in recreation areas, forests, historical sites, state capitals, national monuments, botanic gardens, factories, and other interesting places.

If you stop at a park or highway rest area, you can play the following games and activities. Notice that the toys involved don't take up much space. Most children will already know how to play these games and may even have their own favorite versions:

Tag

Relay Races

(See who can walk holding a leaf on his hand or push a rock with a stick to a goal line the fastest, etc.)

May I?
Simon Says
Duck, Duck, Goose
Red Light, Green Light
Run Sheep Run
Follow The Leader
Statues
Keep Away
Jump Rope
Jacks
Frisbee
Balloon Toss
    (See who can keep it in the air the longest!)
Catch
    (Use an inflatable rubber ball.)
Squirt Gun Fight

In winter make a snowman or play Fox and Geese.

Fox And Geese: In the snow make a large pie shape with six equal divisions. Pick a player to be the "fox." The other players are "geese," and stand somewhere in the paths that have been made. The fox tries to catch the geese, chasing them along the paths. The fox cannot catch the goose in the center free space of the circle. If another goose runs to the center, the goose there must leave or be caught by the fox. If a goose goes out of the paths or gets caught by the fox, it becomes the fox.

If you have trouble getting the kids back in the car after stopping, use a whistle to blow a five-minute warning and then a final come-right-now whistle. This method works better than nagging or losing your voice yelling. You might also tell them about something special you'll be doing next, such as playing a game in the car or heading to a new place to visit. You can also take on the character of a conductor, calling, "All aboard! This train is leaving for _____ and other new and interesting parts unknown."

■ *SEATING AND TIDINESS IN THE CAR* ■

Make a seat rotation plan so everyone gets a chance to sit up front, by the window, or any other choice location. Have a set time to change seats; once an hour is usually about right.

If your children fight over "sides," separate them by putting a toy bag, diaper bag, or small suitcase between them.

A booster seat or car seat will position children higher so they can see out the window and won't get bored or carsick as easily. A suction-cup sun shade on side windows will prevent glare from irritating children's sensitive eyes.

A car will get messy quickly when traveling. Keep your car as clean and tidy as possible so everyone will be more comfortable. Have a place for everything so you can find the items you need quickly and easily. Provide paper towels or a sponge to clean up spills. Better yet, don't eat in the car. Keep a container of wet wipes in the car to clean children's faces and hands.

Use a trash bag, emptying it whenever you stop. My favorite trash bags are the plastic bags you get from grocery stores. They are larger than litter bags and they can be closed by tying the handles together. For more thorough cleaning, you can bring a whisk broom or a small portable vacuum that plugs into the cigarette lighter (though I'm still looking for one that does a good job). Wash your car periodically. Clean windows make driving safer and sight-seeing more pleasant. You also won't dirty your clothes or belongings if you brush against a clean car.

Check store automotive departments for car accessories. You can get spill-resistant cups, tissue and cup holders, cup holders that hang from the window, trash containers, and other conveniences.

■ QUIET TIME AND SLEEP ■

Sometimes a quiet time is needed to restore everyone's nerves. With so much togetherness on vacation, make opportunities for family members to have some privacy. Parents and teenagers especially need time alone.

It's not realistic, however, to expect children to be quiet all the time. The section on quiet games in Chapter 9 offers ideas for games that will keep the atmosphere calm. Soft music will help create a peaceful mood. Story tapes also tend to lower the noise and activity level, whether in a car, in a hotel room, or at the home of a friend or relative.

Everyone needs a good night's sleep to feel good for the day's activities. Daily rest periods should be encouraged for children. Look for opportunities for the children to rest or sleep so they don't become too tired.

If you have very young children, rent a crib or bring a portable, collapsible playpen that can double as a crib. You can improvise a makeshift bed by putting blankets on the floor or by padding a drawer for an infant.

Carry along a small pillow and a small blanket for each child. They are handy for naps and cuddling or keeping warm, especially if you are delayed by traffic or car trouble. A soft, washable pillow can be made easily. Just sew two washcloths together and stuff the resulting pouch with polyester fiberfill.

Before your trip try to get your child used to sleeping in different places so the adjustment isn't difficult. Different surroundings can excite or frighten a child, making bedtime a difficult proposition. Do whatever you can to make children comfortable and secure so they can relax and go to sleep. Provide a favorite cuddly toy or familiar blanket, offer a bottle, read a story, reassure them, and stay close by until they fall asleep. Sometimes the sound of the radio or television will lull overexcited or overtired children to sleep.

A night-light also reassures a child in unfamiliar surroundings and provides enough light to find the light switch or bathroom during the night. In fact, the whole family may benefit from a night-light in a crowded hotel room or unfamiliar home.

■ TOILETING ■

Don't try to potty train a child just before a vacation—the excitement and strangeness of a trip can cause regression. If your child has used a toilet well for several months, take the training pants and see how it goes. Each child will be different. Use a lot of praise each time the child successfully uses a potty. If your child begins to have accidents, avoid scolding or embarrassing remarks; just switch to disposable diapers with reusable tapes. This way you can easily take the child to a restroom, but if there's an accident or a restroom can't be found quickly, there won't be a mess. Keep two diaper pins attached to your key chain in case the reusable tapes won't stick.

The easiest way to avoid frantic searches for a restroom is to have the children use those that are handy *before* someone *has* to go. Every time I think I don't want to be bothered and everyone is fine, ten minutes later when it's terribly inconvenient or the opportunity is gone someone says, "I have to go *right now.*"

If you have your choice of where to stop for a "potty break," try to choose a clean and comfortable place where family members can stretch their legs. Consider bringing a portable toilet seat that folds for a child who's not used to using a toilet or comfortable using a strange one.

Some parents bring a child's portable potty to eliminate the search for restrooms and dealing with strange toilets. You could also keep a plastic bucket or coffee can with a lid in the car to use as a portable toilet for emergencies. The lid prevents spillage and odor until it can be discarded.

■ *BEACH IDEAS* ■

Many families vacation at the beach, a destination both wonderful and difficult for small children. What some families take to the beach they wouldn't need for a month at home. The following tips should make your days at the beach a picnic.

First, pack the sand toys in a mesh bag with a drawstring handle (nylon potato or onion bags are perfect).

They can be carried easily on wrist or stroller handle and quickly replaced at day's end. Then all you have to do is shake or dunk them in the water for cleanup, and they drain and dry easily.

You can make a beach quilt by sewing together old towels to the desired size. This provides a soft, comfortable use for old bath or beach towels. Near your quilt, set up a beach umbrella. Babies and small children need the shade; don't let them sleep in the sun. Small, attachable beach umbrellas will provide shade for a stroller or playpen.

> You may want to use a child wrist hand holder so your toddler doesn't wander away from your spot or into the water.

Wear protective clothing, footwear, and eyewear as well as sunscreens and lip balms. Kids love to wear sunglasses and visors. Sunbonnets and baseball caps also protect their eyes and faces from the sun. Have the family wear thongs, sandals, or beach shoes to protect their feet from the hot sand or broken glass or shells. Bring along T-shirts and beach robes to keep kids warm in cool weather and protect tender skin against the sun. You might consider dressing the kids in T-shirts of the same bright color for the beach. A quick glance lets you find the children. You might also buy bathing suits in one bright color.

Sunblock, especially for fair-skinned children, will prevent the misery of sunburn. Nose and ear creams and lip balm will protect especially vulnerable areas.

Bring water, both to drink and to use for rinsing off sand and salt water before getting in the car. If showers are available, rinse off and then apply baby powder, which blots up moisture and keeps sand from sticking to a just-rinsed child (or adult). If showers are not available, rinse off with your own water. One-liter plastic pop bottles with screw-on lids make nice water bottles.

■ CITY SMARTS ■

Many wonderful sights and experiences are found in the big cities of America—sights your family won't want to miss. Where else would you find the Statue of Liberty, the Smithsonian, or the Golden Gate Bridge, for example? Some knowledge of functioning in a big city is important, however, to make getting around simpler and safer. Of course, it is less complicated if you are visiting friends or relatives who know the ropes and can help you. The following tips will help you enjoy a big-city excursion.

Choose a reputable hotel in a safe area of the city. If you need more than one room, get connecting rooms. Keep your doors locked at all times. Look around . . . if there is anything the least bit unsavory or suspicious outside, then it's not the place for a family to stay. Although it may not be as convenient, you might want to consider staying in the suburbs (usually both safer and less expensive) and commuting to the city.

In the heart of a big city, getting around by car can be very difficult. Parking can be almost nonexistent, and if you find it, very expensive. Splurging on a cab may be well worth it.

Consider taking bus tours as an easy way to sightsee. Also, some cities, such as Honolulu, have wonderful, inexpensive city bus systems that have numerous routes, frequent runs, and helpful drivers.

Ask a friend or hotel personnel about the safety of the subways. There is a difference from city to city. It's wise to stay away during rush hours, when it is easy to lose your children in the crush, or at night, when most subway crime occurs and even city residents stay away.

Know where you are going beforehand, with directions and destinations charted out. It is difficult and dangerous to try to figure out your course on a busy Los Angeles freeway or the streets of Detroit. Keep track of where you are at all times. Don't get so caught up in sightseeing that you wander far from your destination. It is easy to lose your sense of direction among skyscrapers. Learn the street numbering or lettering system if there is one and keep a map of the area with you.

Visit attractions during daylight hours. Some areas are safe in the daytime, but become dangerous after dark. We were in the Los Angeles garment district one wintertime, and a clerk told us, "You're fine now, but get out of here at five o'clock when the stores close and it gets dark because then it's strictly trick-or-treat."

Be cautious and aware of the type of area you are in. What does the area look like? Are there other people on the streets? What type of people are they? Are there other families? Does anything look suspicious or unsafe? If there is a strong police presence and heavy security, there is a reason. Try to stay out of the bad parts of a city; stop only at places that appear safe and well-lit.

Stick together. It's not safe to let children explore on their own. Keep close track of all your children. Agree on a safe place to meet if you are briefly separated. See Chapter 6 for ideas on preventing children from getting lost.

Body language can be very important. Don't gawk or act confused; walk briskly and with an air of purpose and confidence. Don't wear expensive jewelry or pull out a large amount of cash. Remember if approached that your life is more important than your valuables. It's best to leave valuables at home or at least in the hotel safe.

Teach your children not to talk to strangers; tell them how to handle strangers who talk to them. This lesson can be difficult since children are naturally friendly, and some adults love to talk to kids. If you have a baby, people will really take an interest in you. If you avoid eye contact, most people will keep their distance.

CHAPTER 4

Planes and Trains

Planes and Trains

Air Travel

Air travel is a quick and easy way to travel. Air service to thousands of destinations worldwide and connections to other modes of transportation and accommodations make this the method of choice for many traveling families. Many vacation plans offer package deals that include air travel and accommodations at reduced rates. Though more costly than car travel, planes save lots of time at either end of a family vacation.

■ *RESERVATIONS* ■

Make your reservations as soon as possible and obtain tickets, seat assignments, and boarding passes. Be sure to discuss seating, meals, specific needs, or special services. You can deal directly with the airlines or you can use a travel agent.

Travel agents can be helpful because they are professionals. They have the knowledge and information to help you select the right airline, the easiest and fastest route, and the best rates. Best of all, a travel agent doesn't cost you anything.

If you are going to a large city, check to see if you can fly into a smaller airport. This can save a lot of time and hassle. For example, if you fly into Burbank or John Wayne in Orange County, instead of LAX, Los Angeles International, it's easier to find your way around, you receive faster service (especially at peak hours and seasons), parking is usually closer, and traffic is lighter. Small airports aren't as overwhelming to unseasoned travelers.

Try to book your flight during off-peak times like midday and midweek. If the plane is not crowded, you'll have more room for your children. This is especially important if you have a child under two who doesn't have an assigned seat; an underbooked plane will have empty seats that you can use. The attendants will also be able to give you more help and attention.

Depending on the temperament and predictability of your child, you may want to fly during naptime or even at night so that your child can sleep during the flight. You may prefer to fly when your child is awake, refreshed, and alert. In either case, book a nonstop flight directly to your destination. You don't have to cope with changing planes, stopovers, more airports, takeoffs, or landings. Over a long trip, however, it might be beneficial to have a stopover so an active child can run off some energy in the airport terminal.

On a direct flight you won't have to change airplanes, but you will make stops to pick up and let off passengers. These stops can be difficult because you still have the waiting time, making the trip longer and more difficult for children.

On a connecting flight you make one or more stops to change airplanes. Sometimes connections can't be avoided, especially if you are going to or coming from a small airport or have an international destination.

If you have to change flights, allow plenty of time to make the connection, especially if you are changing airlines and going to a different terminal. If time is short, you may need help in making the switch. Ask the reservations manager to help you arrange shuttle cart service, which will take you and/or your luggage to the correct terminal. A gate agent can also direct you to passenger services.

Make sure you are taking the simplest and fastest route. If your flight is delayed, the airline may hold your connecting plane or arrange another connection. If the delay is significant or due to an airline error, you may be entitled to meal or accommodation vouchers at the airline's expense.

On domestic flights children age two and under fly at no charge. They are not assigned a seat, however, and will need to sit on your lap unless an empty seat is available. Reduced fares (25 to 60 percent discounts) are usually offered for children over two years. Children age twelve and over pay adult fare. Excursion or promotional rates are offered from time to time, providing significant savings. Restrictions often apply, so check your options thoroughly. You may save a great deal by traveling at off-peak seasons and just before or after national holidays.

> Always call the airline before leaving home to make sure your flight is on schedule. Then, if your flight is delayed, you can wait at home with the children instead of at the airport.

Get to the airport at least an hour (hour and a half if it's a busy time of year) before your flight so you have time to confirm your seats, check your bags, and get settled. A reserved seat usually needs to be claimed at least fifteen to thirty minutes before takeoff. If the seat is not claimed, the airline will reassign it.

■ *BOARDING* ■

It takes longer to board with children, especially if you are checking sports equipment or car seats. Don't try to cut it close—you will frazzle your nerves and maybe miss your flight. On the other hand, don't get there too soon or you will have too much time to spend in the terminal.

Airports are exciting places for children. They love to watch all the activity, and the planes landing and taking off. Remember to tell them what to expect at the airport and the proper behavior expected from them on the plane. Within reason, let your children exercise in the airport, especially if you have a long flight ahead of you.

You'll save time and energy if you can split the jobs with a spouse or other adult. While one of you is checking baggage or car seats, the other can take the kids to the restroom, to the snack bar, or to the departure gate. Remember children hate to wait in lines.

Let the gate agent know you have children, and the airline will allow you to board first. Early boarding allows you to get settled in and stow your carry-on luggage close to your seat.

If you have a restless child, you might want to have one adult board last with the child to provide extra time to exercise before being confined to a seat.

See Chapter 6 on child safety for ideas to prevent children from becoming lost in airports. Young children can wear wrist hand holders so that they can walk alone and your hands are left free to carry luggage. You might also want to put identification tags in children's clothing or shoes.

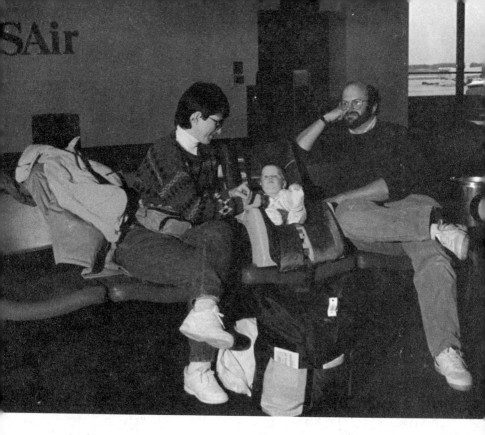

Airline personnel are trained to watch for lost children, and they will help locate parents and children. If a child is lost, go immediately to a gate agent and request help.

■ *LUGGAGE* ■

Take as little carry-on luggage as possible when you have small children to hold and watch. Tag all your luggage with your name, business address, and home phone number. Add a destination address that will tell the airline where to send your luggage if it gets lost.

Don't put your home address on the outside of luggage because thieves will watch luggage tags to find the addresses of people who are not home. Some travelers like to slip their business cards in the tag holder.

Put an identification tag that includes your home address inside your suitcase in case the outside tag comes off and your luggage gets lost. Make sure previous destination tags have been removed to avoid confusion. Check to see that the airline personnel put the proper destination tag on your luggage so it lands in the same airport you do.

It's a good idea to mark your luggage in a unique way since a lot of luggage looks the same. Then you can spot it quickly, and it won't be mistakenly picked up by someone else. You can attach a yarn tassel or ribbon to the handles. Stickers or colored tape can also be put on the sides of your luggage.

One carry-on bag can be packed for the whole family, or each child can bring one. Backpacks, athletic bags, drawstring or zipper bags, or any kind of satchel that has a handle and a secure snap or zipper will make a good flight bag. Avoid bringing toys that can roll under seats, are noisy, or have small pieces that can get lost easily.

Pack money, jewelry, or other valuables in a bag you carry with you. Don't pack them inside checked luggage. The carry-on bag should include items to entertain and comfort the family while on the plane as well as anything that might be needed to hold you over for a few days in case of airline delays or lost luggage. This is especially important during bad weather, busy holidays, and summer months. See Chapter 2 for a checklist of items you might consider packing in carry-on luggage.

Car Seats: You may bring a car seat for your child to use if it is approved by the Federal Aviation Administration. You may use it if there is an empty seat if the child is flying free, or if you've paid for a seat. If there isn't a seat available, the attendant will stow it or have it checked for you. When making your reservations check the airline's policy on seating infants and toddlers. Car seats may not be allowed in certain seats, such as near emergency doors or exits. While most major car seat manufacturers have approval from the FAA, check the label on your unit to be sure it is an approved seat.

Using a car seat can be an advantage because it is more comfortable for you and the child and provides a familiar place for the child to sleep. Your child will be safer in a car seat than on your lap if you encounter air turbulence. Since you'll need it for car travel when you reach your destination, you might as well take it aboard.

Umbrella Strollers are also very useful in airports and at your destination. You can hang your carry-on bag on the handles, and the stroller can usually be carried on the plane and hung in the coat rack.

■ *SEATING* ■

If you can book a flight that originates in your city, you will have a better seat selection. If possible, try to reserve your seats when you make your flight reservations. You will want to choose seats that fit your needs and allow you immediate access to the children. Separated seats will *not* work well with children younger than teens. Two-parent families should try to arrange seating that allows both parents to manage the children.

Many people traveling with children request the bulkhead seats because they have more legroom, which gives you more space to take care of a child. There are no seats in front of you, and therefore no people to disturb. Unfortunately, bulkhead seats have several disadvantages. First, there is no convenient under-seat storage space (only overhead compartments). Also, meal trays may be positioned in such a way that feeding a child may be difficult. On a jumbo jet, the side-aisle bulkhead seats are close to the emergency exits where children cannot sit. The center-aisle bulkhead seats are available for children, but are located close to the restrooms, which may mean a line of people will be waiting their turn around you. In addition, bulkhead seats do not fully recline and their armrests are not removable for naptime.

Aisle seats provide more legroom than window or center seats, and if you need to take children for a walk or to the restroom, you won't have to climb over other people. Aisle and window seats provide more diversion for active children. They can look out the window and move around more easily than in center seats. If you are nursing a baby, a window or bulkhead seat will give you more privacy. Emergency regulations require that only one infant can be seated in a row.

You will probably be most comfortable if you seat your family with parents placed between children. You might consider aisle seats across from each other, or window seats with part of the family seated in the row behind the others. Put one parent or adult with each child or group of children. If you are traveling with another adult and a child under two years, ask for the aisle and window seats in a three-seat row. Leave the middle seat empty and hope that no other passenger takes it. If the plane is full, the occupant of the middle seat will usually gladly trade seats with you so you can sit together.

Some parents like to choose seats close to the flight attendants. They are close by when you need assistance, and their activities sometimes entertain children.

■ ON BOARD ■

When you make your reservations, ask the airline about any special services or amenities they have. Many airlines carry a variety of items for the entertainment of children. Junior pilot wings, flight certificates, activity or coloring books, crayons, playing cards, postcards, small toys, games, and puzzles are usually provided at no extra charge. Kids enjoy the novelty of these treats, and attendants are usually more than happy to help your kids get settled before they are busy serving snacks or meals. Special children's menus are available on most domestic flights and many international flights. Request them when you make your reservations. If you get to the airport early, ask the flight crew if your children can see the cockpit. In-flight movies and radio stations are good entertainment for older children. Some airlines have special music stations for children. If you're lucky, the music will lull little ones to sleep.

Changes in the air pressure during takeoff and landing can cause pain and pressure in children's ears. Sucking, chewing, swallowing, or yawning can help relieve the pressure and discomfort. Give an older child a piece of gum or something chewy to eat. A baby can nurse or suck on a bottle or pacifier. If your child has a cold, ask your doctor to recommend a decongestant that you can give before the flight. If ear discomfort is a real problem, try soaking paper towels in hot water, stuffing them in a paper cup, and holding the cup up against the ear to provide relief.

Airsickness may affect young and infrequent flyers. Before you leave home, ask your physician to suggest or prescribe motion sickness medication. Sometimes these medications will cause drowsiness, which in this case can be helpful for children. You can also try to prevent airsickness by eating lightly before flying, getting fresh air from the overhead air vent, sitting in the nonsmoking section, avoiding stimulants like coffee, tea, and alcohol, and sitting in the rows in front of the wings where the plane is less affected by air turbulence. When you are seated, check to see that you have airsickness bags in the seat pockets. If they are missing, ask the flight attendant for them. Don't wait until you need them!

Meals are usually served on flights of more than two hours; snacks are provided on shorter flights. When you make your reservations check to see if a meal will be served. Many airlines have a separate children's menu with typical kids' fare as well as vegetarian, low-fat, and diabetic options. You must request any of these special baby or children's meals at the time you make your reservation. These meals can be exciting for children because of the special tray, table, and containers. Some airlines don't have or only stock emergency baby food and formula, so be sure to check ahead of time. Snacks may include cheese and crackers, peanuts, milk, juices, and soft drinks. You might want to bring other snacks to munch on in case of delays or your own food if you have a fussy eater.

When you make your reservations, find out the arrival times (as closely as possible!) so you can plan your baby's feeding. Ask about handling the preparation, refrigeration, and warming of baby bottles. When you board, let the flight attendant know your needs.

Airplane restrooms are small at best and only a parent and a very small child will be able to use one together. Take the children to the restroom in the airport before you board and change the baby's diaper in the boarding area. Make sure you bring plenty of diapers. The airlines may carry extra in case of emergencies, but you should have an ample supply of your own. Diapering is nearly impossible in a plane restroom, so don't be too shy about diapering your child in the cabin. If you only have a wet diaper, you can usually change it on your lap in your seat without upsetting anyone. Ask the flight attendant for advice on changing a dirty diaper. A very young infant can be changed on your lap in the restroom, but it would be much easier to change infants as well as toddlers on the floor of the galley or in the attendants' jumpseats. Dispose of diapers properly; rinse and flush solid waste. Don't leave soiled diapers in the seat pockets, of course.

If you are taking a long flight, you are probably hoping your children will sleep at least part of the time. Babies are usually lulled to sleep by the noise of the plane's engines. Some airlines have bassinets for small babies; they are usually free, but you must reserve them ahead of time. Find out if they go on the floor or are attached to the bulkhead seats (in which case you will have to reserve those seats). If there are empty seats available, you can lift the armrest so a child can lie down and stretch out. The seats will recline for sleep or rest, except those in front of the emergency or exit rows. The bulkhead seats will not fully recline, and the armrests cannot be removed.

If you want your children to sleep, choose seats away from noisy, busy areas like the galley and restrooms. You also might want to choose seating separate from your other children to allow a child to sleep undisturbed. If you can get a child to sleep, it will be easier for both of you. Airlines have blankets and pillows available in the overhead storage or upon request. Request them and get your child settled before the lights are turned out for a movie, since sometimes children will fall asleep during that time. If the flight is full, request blankets or pillows before they are all taken.

■ DEPLANING ■

Don't rush to be the first one off the plane. It will be easier if you wait until the other passengers have left because you won't have to be jostled around with children in a crowded aisle. The flight attendants will also be freer to help you. In the end it won't matter anyway since you'll have to wait for your baggage.

Jet lag occurs when your body's biological clock is different from the one on the wall, thereby upsetting sleep, hunger, and other body functions. Jet lag is caused by crossing several or more time zones in a short period of "real" time. The more time zones you cross, the longer it will take your body to recover. Flying west lengthens your day, and flying east shortens it. Because flying east compresses the day/night cycle, it is harder to make the adjustment.

Jet lag may include symptoms such as headache, nausea, lightheadedness, apathy, irritability, fatigue, and insomnia. While nothing will eliminate the need for your body to adjust, you can try to reduce the effects by beginning your adjustment to the new time a few days before the trip. Eat and go to sleep earlier for west-to-east travel or later for east-to-west travel. Try to have everyone well rested before your flight and reduce the stress on your body by eating and exercising moderately, dressing comfortably, and resting or sleeping on the plane if possible. Don't drink stimulants like coffee, tea, or alcohol. Allow time for your body to recover by taking it easy the first few days in the new time zone. Current research indicates exposure to sunlight helps the body readjust faster, so enjoy outdoor activities at your destination if you can. Go to bed by the time on the wall, not by your body clock. Allow a baby or small child to feed on demand for a while until an adjustment to the new time is made. Eating schedules will adjust faster than sleep patterns.

Train Travel

Like air travel, train travel offers moderately fast service to a great number of destinations, and similarly, you may be able to enjoy the scenery while someone else does the driving. Children seem to love trains, and many families take to the rails for family vacations. Amtrak in the United States and VIA in Canada provide service to cities and recreation areas across the continent. Smaller interstate or intrastate railways also offer services for shorter trips. Amtrak's Auto Train provides transportation for families (and their cars) traveling between Washington, DC, and Orlando, Florida; the Metroliner offers high-speed service between New York and Washington; and the bi-level superliners feature coach cars, sightseeing lounges, and a great variety of accommodations and amenities. Hotel packages and further transportation connections can be arranged through Amtrak and VIA.

Vacation tours offer on-board movies, taped music programs, and occasional cartoons for children. Complimentary snacks, hospitality hours, and games such as bingo and trivia are offered on some trains. Reclining seats, overhead storage, reading lights, and pillows are offered on all Amtrak and VIA trains. They also have dining cars, snack bars or cafe cars, and of course restrooms. Most trains allow two pieces of carry-on luggage per passenger; all other luggage is checked (unless you have reserved a sleeping compartment, in which case you can bring aboard any luggage that will fit in your room). Assistance is available from train attendants and from Red Cap luggage handlers; many stations also have free or low-cost handcarts for your use.

You can call Amtrak or VIA for information on items such as car seats, strollers, bicycles or other sports equipment, and musical instruments. Call Amtrak at 1-800-USA-RAIL to obtain prices, reservations, and a copy of its brochure "National Train Timetables" (lists routes, schedules, services, and connecting bus services). Amtrak also publishes a free travel guide called *Discover the Magic: Amtrak's America,* which describes vacation packages, accommodations, reservations and fare information, special tours, and services for physically challenged passengers. It provides tips for traveling with children, handling baggage, overnight travel, meals, and includes suggestions on what to do on board. The transcontinental Canadian railway, VIA, also publishes guides and timetables. Call (800) 561-3949.

Fares for children ages two through eleven are half the price of the adult fare; children under age two are free. As in airline travel, a seat is not reserved for a child under age two. Check to see if a special reduced or promotional fare is available by calling Amtrak or your travel agent.

A night train offers you the opportunity to get where you're going while the family sleeps, enjoying a full day of activities in one destination and then, in the morning, in another. Sleeping accommodations and meals are offered at additional cost; many packages and options are offered. If you purchase sleeping accommodations, meals are included in the price. On Amtrak, children's menus are available, as are vegetarian, kosher, and low-salt meals (call Special Services for information). Different services and accommodations are available on different routes. Prices will vary according to the accommodations and the food and beverage service you choose. If you reserve a sleeping compartment, all linens and pillows are provided along with a towel, soap, and a goodnight treat. Beverages and a newspaper are often offered along with your morning wake-up call, and breakfast is served in the dining car. Deluxe accommodations include private toilet and shower facilities.

On long distance trains, tickets must be reserved in advance, especially during busy holiday or vacation periods. All seating is assigned, but passengers are free to visit the lounges or dining cars. Children can watch cartoons, movies, or television in the lounge. Most trains have picture windows that allow you to look out and watch the scenery; some trains have glass-topped dome cars. As with other travel, you will need to bring along some activities to help entertain your children. Playing cards and postcards are available on some trains. A small blanket and extra snacks are helpful.

If desired, request a nonsmoking car when you make your reservations. Ask where and how often you will change trains or have layovers. Ask if your luggage will be checked through so you don't have to pick it up until your destination.

For local trains, arrive early enough to obtain desirable seats since seating is on a first-come, first-service basis. Remember that few or no amenities are offered on local commuter railways.

CHAPTER 5

Let's Eat

Let's Eat

Part of the fun on vacation is eating snacks, picnicking, eating out, and sampling the local cuisine. The key to success is to be flexible; adapt yourself to different needs and situations. Since no one way is the right way even on the same trip, this chapter provides a variety of ideas to help you enjoy vacation meals.

Be sure to take into account each person's preferences. If you consider eating out an important experience of the trip, then take the time necessary to enjoy it. If it isn't important, then find ways to cut some of the time it takes to eat by carrying prepared meals, or eating sandwiches or fast food.

In my experience a vacation isn't a vacation if you're constantly preparing food. Even if you travel in an RV, go to a restaurant sometimes for a change and give the chef a break.

When you need to eat, stop if at all possible so family members can get out of the car to stretch their legs and release excess energy. You can stop at a park, a campground, a national monument, or other point of interest. Of course, you can't stop every time someone wants a snack or you might not even make it out of town!

■ EATING IN THE CAR ■

If you've ever allowed the family to eat in the car, you know you vowed never to do it again. It is not easy to clean up a car after a meal, and french fries have been known to appear months later.

If you do need to eat in the car, use shoe boxes to hold your food. A shoe box will contain the mess, and the kids can hold and balance their own meals without needing constant help. If you do this often, get plastic shoe boxes that you can clean and reuse. When you're done, wipe them out and stack them together.

Serve drinks in individual packages or cans so you don't have to pour from a bottle. There's always a bump or turn in the road at the wrong moment!

If you like to eat ice-cream bars or popsicles, cut a slit in the middle of a small paper plate and insert the stick through the slit. The plate will catch most of the drips.

For easy cleanup, use disposable wet wipes and plastic or disposable bibs. Put newspapers or an old towel under the car seat or cover the back seat of the car with a beach towel. Bring a sponge for quick wipe-ups.

■ *EATING SCHEDULES* ■

Use a schedule that will work best for your family, but remember to eat as regularly as possible. A hungry family is always a cross one. If your children are sensitive to changes, try not to alter their diet too much on vacation; stick to foods they are used to. If your children don't usually eat a big breakfast, don't eat in a restaurant where the food, your time, and money will be wasted. Try a small, quick continental breakfast. You can also travel or sightsee for an hour or so, and have breakfast when they're more hungry.

Many families save time and money by eating only two meals a day plus snacks when traveling. If you are sitting in a car for long periods, you don't need or burn the calories from three meals and snacks. I've come home from some trips with not only memories, but extra pounds!

You might consider picnics for breakfast and dinner. Make the noon meal your largest. Lunch at a restaurant is less expensive than dinner, and there is less social pressure on the kids then, as well. Have your meals before the usual rush hours so you don't have to wait as long for service, and the waitress will be able to give the kids more attention.

■ PICNICKING ■

Remember that a restaurant is as confining as a car or other transportation to a child. Picnics allow the children a chance to get outdoors. A picnic break is restful and will seem twice as long as the same amount of time in a restaurant.

Picnics help you avoid fast-food burnout, give you more control over your diet, and are a good way to save money. They're also convenient. You can stop and eat when you want to, and you have the security of knowing you have your own food supply if you're out in the middle of nowhere. Take some food with you from home, and restock at grocery stores as you travel.

Picnicking can be done easily with some simple but necessary preparations. The basic supplies you will need are a cooler, a picnic supply box, and food. A one-burner stove can be handy for more elaborate meals. The picnic supply box should be stocked with basics such as paper goods, condiments, a plastic tablecloth, a can opener, and a knife. (See Chapter 2 for a complete list.) Keep this box handy for all trips, replacing or cleaning any used items when you arrive home.

I find it saves frustration, indecision, and overpacking if I make up menus before we leave our home. Delegate some of the responsibilities for food preparation and cleanup so Mom isn't always stuck with those chores. Keep your picnicking simple unless it is the main focus of the trip, and there is ample time for extra efforts.

Take foods that can be eaten easily. Picnic lunches work best with foods such as sandwich fixings (bread, butter, fillings like cheese, peanut butter, bologna), potato or corn chips, cold drinks, fruit, salads, canned pudding, or cookies. If you have a one-burner stove or hot plate, you can heat canned foods like vegetables, soups, chili, spaghetti, or instant ready-to-mix foods. Avoid leftovers since they are hard to carry and keep fresh.

Breakfast is the easiest meal to handle. You can eat it in a motel room or a park. Cold cereal is easy if you use individual, foil-lined boxes, which can be used as bowls. A continental breakfast of sweet rolls or donuts, fresh fruit, and milk or juice in small cartons is especially easy and portable.

■ *SNACKS* ■

Even if you plan to eat all your meals in a restaurant, take a cooler with snacks. You can also chill food in a motel ice bucket.

Snacks provide ready refreshment, help pass the time, and help calm cross children. Kids get hungry more often than adults, and a snack can relieve a frantic search for a restaurant.

Keep small treats in your purse, glove compartment, or backpack. These can really tide you over when a child is bored, tired, or irritable. This is especially true with small children when nothing will make them happy. On one trip, doling out a few raisins per room was the only trick that got me through the Hearst Castle with a cross three-year-old.

Keep food in plastic, resealable zip-type bags. If you use individual bags, you can distribute individual treats or snacks easily. Pack a small knife to cut up fruit or divide larger snacks into small pieces.

When choosing food to bring along, don't take foods that are messy or sticky. Avoid foods that melt, crumble, stain, or drip. Candy can be one of the worst culprits. Avoid chocolate, suckers, or anything your children have a tendency to taste and take back out of their mouths. My favorite candy to bring is licorice.

Avoid taking too many salty or sweet foods that will make the kids thirsty and thereby require more restroom stops later. Too many sweets can upset stomachs and spoil dinners, so take nutritious snacks along with special treats. Oranges and grapes will combat hunger and thirst. Gum will help you cope with air pressure changes that occur on the road or in the air.

You can make special treats by combining several kinds of dry cereal, small crackers, raisins, nuts, or candy-coated chocolate pieces in small plastic bags. These are easy to serve and provide a variety of different foods to eat.

You might want to take a snack break, stopping to buy popsicles, ice cream, or locally grown fruit or vegetables (if sanitation isn't a problem). Ice cream is nutritious and refreshing, and the stop gives everyone a chance to stretch.

The best on-the-road snacks for kids are:

fruits: apples, bananas, grapes, oranges
dried fruit, raisins
beef jerky
trail mix
granola and fruit bars
nuts
vegetables: carrot and celery sticks
boiled eggs
cheese
yogurt
pudding
crackers
popcorn
dry cereal
cookies
rolls/muffins/bagels
candy/gum
sodas, juices, milk
    (in boxes, pouches, cans)

■ *DRINKING WATER* ■

Water is the best beverage to order or take along. It's not messy when spilled (with kids it's a matter of when, not if) and your children usually won't ask for unnecessary drinks just for the taste or diversion.

My favorite way to carry water is in an air pump thermos, which doesn't need to be tipped to dispense the water and can be used easily in a moving car.

A good method of keeping cold water on hand the first few days of your trip is to fill a plastic gallon jug three-quarters full of water; freeze it, then add tap water to the top when you're ready to leave. The water will stay cold, and as the ice melts you'll have more cold water to drink. You can also put the jug in your cooler to double as an ice pack.

Give children their own differently colored, collapsible cups to use only for water. Put them in their activity bags so they can find and use them easily. This will cut down on paper cups strewn all over the car. You can also use plastic squirt or sport bottles as individual drinking bottles (you can freeze water in these).

Since water differs from one place to another, you might want to buy bottled drinking water for a baby or sensitive child. Even good water may cause diarrhea or an upset stomach if it is different from the water at home.

■ *RESTAURANTS* ■

Whenever possible, call restaurants ahead of time to check if reservations are needed or suggested, the type of food served, price range, hours, directions, and suitability for children. Ask if a children's menu or high chairs are available.

Before you stop at a restaurant, explain what will happen (younger children don't understand why it isn't like at home), and the behavior that is expected. Babies should be fed first so you can enjoy your meal. Let the children exercise a bit before entering the restaurant. One adult can order the food while the other takes the kids for a walk. Waiting is hard for children, and this will save you the stress of entertaining and controlling them. Be sure to use the restroom for washing hands and faces and toileting; then your dinner won't be interrupted by separate or en masse visits to the restrooms.

It's easier to handle children in an out-of-the-way booth, rather than at tables in the middle of a restaurant. Let a toddler sit facing a window, where cars and people will be interesting to watch.

If you have a toddler, ask for a high chair or booster seat, a children's menu, a disposable bib, extra napkins or towelettes, and crackers. Remove items that can break or cause injury.

You can make your own restaurant kit in a small shoe box, pencil box, or zippered bag; include small utensils, towelettes, crackers, small toys, a high chair belt, and bibs. Keep a length of ribbon or yarn and two paper clamps in your purse or backpack to make a bib if none are available. Attach each end of ribbon or yarn to the clamps and clip

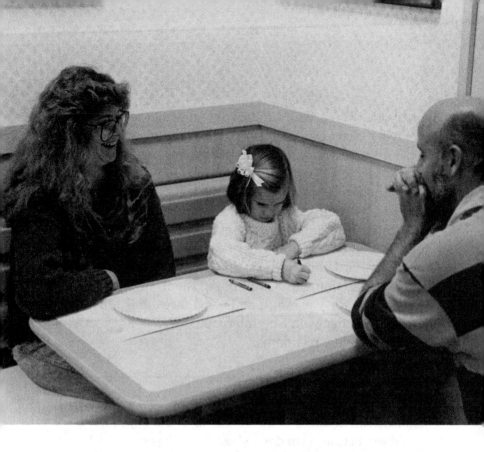

them onto a napkin or paper towel, making a disposable bib. You can also keep two large safety pins attached to your key chain and use them to pin a napkin to a child's shirt.

If you need to entertain children while waiting for your food, let them take a small toy to play with quietly (use a toy they are not already bored with). Teach them what the workers do at the restaurant, or play word and quiet games from the game section of this book. Kids may also enjoy playing with a few crayons or a pencil and paper. Paper napkins or paper place mats can also be used as a writing surface. Sometimes the restaurant will have special toys or printed place mats for children. Let the children know that toys must be put away when the food arrives.

Food Basket is an amusing food game to play in a restaurant. Have one player choose a food category like fruit. Each player in turn then names a fruit. When someone can't think of a different fruit or repeats one that has already been used, that player is out of that round. The player staying in the longest is the winner and selects the next category. Possible categories are drinks, breads, fruits, vegetables, meats, main dishes, or desserts.

Many times children's appetites will dwindle on a trip. Try to order familiar foods they like and steer them toward items that can be put in a doggie bag easily. We all know that a child who is "not hungry" will be "starving" as soon as you've left the restaurant! You can share bread, rolls, fruit, and other finger foods with a small child.

Traveling is a good opportunity for the older members of your family to try special regional foods. A few examples are: salmon and crab in the Northwest; avocados and artichokes in California; trout in the Rockies; sopapillas and Mexican food in the Southwest; barbecue, salsa, and beans in Texas; Chicago stuffed pizza and Cincinnati chili in the Midwest; Hoppin' John (rice and black-eyed peas), Creole foods, grits, and hush puppies in the South; shrimp on the Gulf Coast; Boston baked beans, chowder, Indian pudding, and lobster in New England; and deli corned beef and cheesecake in New York; the list goes on and on! Sampling local fare can be an educational experience.

Be careful about introducing young children to new foods such as shellfish or spicy foods. Although vacation is a good time to experiment with new tastes, serve only a small amount at first in case the child doesn't like the dish or has an allergic reaction.

Clean children's sticky hands and faces before you leave the restaurant, and remember to compliment them on what they did well.

■ FEEDING THE BABY ■

Don't try to make any major changes in a baby's diet just before a trip. Don't start new foods or wean from breast to bottle or bottle to cup. I would, however, encourage you to persuade an older baby to take a cooler temperature bottle so that you won't have the difficulty of trying to warm bottles. Before your trip, make baby's bottle a little bit cooler each day. I don't like to do this with a small baby since it seems to upset the stomach.

Nursing mothers will have an easier time on vacation—no cans or bottles to bring, no warming or refrigerating prepared formula.

If your baby is formula-fed, try to make the process as easy as possible. The easiest (but most expensive) method is to bring cans or bottles of ready-to-serve formula that don't need refrigeration. Put the can or bottle in the sun to warm or place it in a wide-mouth thermos filled with hot water. The water in the thermos can also be used for cleanup.

My favorite way is to premeasure powdered formula in bottles, making *very* sure there is no moisture in the bottle. Add warm water from a thermos or a tap to complete the job.

If you are only going for a short trip, bacteria growth will not be a problem, so you can put the water in the bottles and add the powdered formula when you need to feed baby. If you use bottles with plastic disposable liners, you'll have less cleanup to do.

Ready-to-use juices are convenient since all you need to do is take off the lid and screw on a nipple set. You can also purchase ready-to-use cereal in jars, or pack baby cereal premixed with powdered formula in individual, resealable bags or baby food jars. All you have to do is add warm water and serve.

Don't bring a baby food grinder on vacation. It can be nice to use at home, but is too messy to use and clean on the road. Make your trip easier by buying prepared fruits and vegetables in jars. They are small, easy to use, and don't have to be refrigerated unless they have been opened.

Instead of bringing along child-size utensils that need to be washed, get some small plastic spoons to use instead. You can tape one to each baby food jar for quick use, so you don't have to hunt all over for a spoon.

If handled well, eating on vacation can be a pleasurable experience with special food and treats that become part of the memories. Plan ahead so mealtime is a happy experience for your family.

Health and Safety

Health and Safety

In this chapter you'll read some down-to-earth suggestions that will help keep your family safe and healthy. Health information is included to help you avoid getting sick; illnesses that you would not usually worry about at home sometimes occur on vacation. Information can be more difficult to obtain away from home, so it's a good idea to take a first-aid kit and a good first aid book.

The information in this chapter is offered as a general help and guide for the common problems encountered while traveling. It is not meant to replace the advice and treatment of a medical doctor. If you have any questions, contact a competent medical doctor for advice and treatment.

■ *PRECAUTIONS* ■

If someone in your family has an illness, medical condition, or tendency toward any medical problems that might need attention while traveling, discuss the situation with your doctor before you go. Ask the doctor to write down any important information another doctor would want to know about the history or treatment of the problem. Clear information will aid a doctor unfamiliar with the patient and will help you obtain proper care.

It is also a good idea to obtain an extra written prescription for necessary medications in case you lose or run out of what you need. A prescription for eyeglass lenses will help in case of loss or breakage. Ask your doctor about any medications or remedies you should use

for such common travel problems as motion sickness and diarrhea.

Know or take records of each family member's blood type, any medications currently being taken, allergies to medications, and other pertinent health information. Make sure you know how to administer treatment for any disorder they may have.

Take your doctor's name and telephone number and your insurance company name, telephone number, policy number, identification cards, and claim forms. Health insurance companies have specific policies you must follow to obtain coverage for your medical expenses. Before you leave home, find out the procedure to follow if you need medical care for an illness, an injury, or a life-threatening emergency away from home. Also ask if you need special authorization or forms.

If you are traveling within the United States or Canada and need medical care, it is usually easiest and safest to contact a hospital emergency room. Since hospital care is usually more expensive than a private doctor, ask for a reference to a qualified local doctor if the situation is not an emergency.

If you are traveling abroad, medical care and facilities will vary in different countries. Contact the nearest American embassy or consulate for information on obtaining medical care.

Whenever you receive medical treatment obtain a signed, written statement indicating the illness or injury, diagnosis, treatment, medications prescribed, and the itemized costs. This record will be useful for your information and insurance purposes when you return home.

■ COMMON COMPLAINTS ■

Food Poisoning

To help prevent food poisoning, be careful about the foods you eat on your trip. Tainted foods don't always look, taste, or smell bad. If the food is questionable, don't eat it. The following safety guidelines will help you avoid food poisoning when you are traveling in areas where sanitation and food handling are a concern.

Eat only foods that are washed, cooked, or that you can peel yourself. Since heat kills germs, food or liquids that are served and kept hot at proper temperatures are usually safe. Don't order foods that can spoil easily, especially foods prepared ahead of time, cold dishes and salads made with mayonnaise, fish, meats, eggs, cheese, or dairy products. Drink only pasteurized milk or milk products that you can get in well-chilled containers. Order red meats and poultry well done. Stay away from seafood, most especially shellfish, if you question the freshness or handling of the catch. Refrain, especially, from offering children shellfish if they are not accustomed to it; adverse reactions are common.

Food poisoning can cause nausea, cramps, fever, chills, vomiting, and diarrhea. It can begin six to forty-eight hours after the contaminated food is eaten and may continue for several days. The cause and severity will determine how long the attack will last.

With the exception of ice chips and sips of water, refrain from eating or drinking anything until the vomiting stops. Progress gradually to easily digested foods such as gelatin and toast. Consult a doctor if the attack is severe or the victim is young or elderly. A severe attack may include a high fever, vomiting for more than twelve hours, signs of nerve or muscle paralysis, double vision, respiratory failure, or difficulty swallowing or breathing.

Diarrhea

Diarrhea is usually caused by changes in drinking water, new or different foods, excess amounts of fruits or juice, illness, tension, change of routine, or the excitement of your trip. There is a higher probability of diarrhea developing on a trip because the bacteria in the food and water may be different from those your body usually encounters. Small amounts of bacteria might affect a child more than an adult.

In high risk areas where water sanitation is not good, the best way to prevent diarrhea and other water-borne illness is to drink bottled water. Don't swallow bath or shower water or use tap water to brush your teeth; don't make ice cubes with tap water or buy locally made ice.

Symptoms are frequent, watery bowel movements; you may also experience nausea, vomiting, headache, cramps, and fever. Diarrhea usually lasts one to three days. Whatever the cause of diarrhea, don't ignore it. It's better to slow down, rest, and eat lightly to give the body a chance to recover.

Serious diarrhea can lead to dehydration. Drink a lot of clear liquids or carbonated soft drinks to replace body fluids. Ease back into your normal diet. Avoid milk products, spicy foods, fruit, alcohol, and coffee for several days after the attack. Be more moderate in the foods you eat, and cut back on rich, spicy foods.

Be sure to consult a doctor if you are uncertain of the cause of the attack, or if it is severe or unresponsive to treatment. If the stool contains blood or mucus or is accompanied by vomiting or fever, you will need medical attention. If the sufferer is elderly or a baby or small child, a doctor's care is advised, especially if any other medical condition is present.

Constipation

Constipation can be caused by stress, new types of food, change in toilet habits, not enough fruits, juices or bulky foods, or insufficient physical activity.

Foods that can help relieve constipation are whole grains, dried fruits, raw fruits or vegetables, prunes, apricots, juices, and lots of water. Stay away from refined foods; eat foods that supply roughage. It is helpful to relax, take time for regular bowel movements, and exercise daily.

Consult a doctor if constipation persists or if dark blood is seen in the stool.

Sunburn

Sunburn is caused by overexposure to the sun's rays. The skin reddens, then burns. If exposure increases, swelling and blisters can appear. Sunburns are usually painful and may cause fever and headache.

A sunburn may be acquired even as you sit in the shade or play outdoors on an overcast or foggy day, particularly if you are around water. Water and other outdoor surfaces such as cement, sand, and asphalt reflect and intensify the sun's rays. Sunburn can be acquired by reflection of the sun on snow. The sun can burn you through light clothing, especially if it is wet. If you are in the water, the sun's rays can pass through water, increasing your sun exposure.

The risk of sunburn is greatest between 10:00 A.M. and 3:00 P.M. The nearer you are to the equator and the higher your altitude, the greater your chance of suffering a burn. A tan can provide some natural protection, but the skin is still susceptible to damage from the sun.

Don't judge how much sun you have gotten by how burned or tan you look. It can take several hours or more after exposure to the sun for the full sunburn to show.

The most effective way to prevent sunburn is to stay out of the sun during high risk hours and to use sunscreen and protective clothing. Wear a hat to protect your head and hair. The eyes should be protected with sunglasses since sun damage can be especially painful to the eyes. If you must be in the sun during midday, limit your exposure as much as possible, gradually increasing it as your skin builds up protection.

If a sunburn occurs, watch for signs of dehydration and heat exhaustion. Medical care should be sought for severe cases. First aid for the skin is the same as for any other burn. Cool baths, resting in a cool room, and sucking on ice chips will increase comfort. Drink a lot of water and a few salty crackers to replace fluid and salt loss.

Heat Exhaustion

Consider the heat when planning your activities. Overexposure to the sun can cause complications that may spoil your vacation. To help avoid heat problems, stay cool and avoid strenuous outdoor activity during midday. Cover up with a hat and loose, lightweight, light colored clothing.

Eat lightly and drink plenty of liquids. Avoid alcohol, which tends to dehydrate the body.

Heat exhaustion is caused by exposure to heat and overexertion, resulting in depletion of the body's salt and fluids. It is fairly common, but its symptoms may be vague at first. Look for nausea, headache, vomiting, sweating, and feelings of weakness, dizziness, or fatigue. The skin may appear cool, pale, and moist; the body temperature is normal or below normal.

Heat exhaustion can usually be treated by moving the patient to a cool place (avoid chilling the patient, however), and loosening tight clothing. Apply wet, cool cloths and have the patient lie down with feet slightly elevated. Give sips of salt water (one teaspoon of salt per glass) or eat salty foods like crackers to replace salts lost through perspiration.

Nausea will usually subside after resting. Medical care may be necessary if there is vomiting or if the heat exhaustion is severe.

Heat exposure can also lead to sunstroke. Sunstroke symptoms are a high body temperature; rapid, pounding pulse; lack of perspiration; hot, red, dry skin; and sometimes unconsciousness. Medical care is needed immediately!

Frostbite

Frostbite is caused by exposure to extreme cold. The nose, ears, and cheeks are the most susceptible body parts since they are the least protected. With frostbite the skin is cold, hard, and white, with no feeling.

The victim should be taken out of the cold and given warm fluids to drink. Circulation should be carefully reestablished by rewarming the frosted body part by immersion in warm (body temperature, *not* hot) water. If this is not possible, use the body heat by wrapping the patient in warm blankets. Do not use intense heat such as a hot water bottle or heat lamp; do not rub the area manually or with snow as this increases tissue damage. The frostbitten areas are sometimes painful while being rewarmed. When circulation is reestablished, have the patient exercise fingers and toes. Do not break any blisters. Protect breaks in the skin with a sterile dressing to avoid infection.

Hypothermia

This condition is caused by overexposure to the cold. Aggravated by wetness, wind, and exhaustion, hypothermia occurs when your body loses heat faster than it produces it. In early stages, exercise and shivering will help you stay warm, and your body adjusts to preserve the normal temperature of vital organs. Prolonged exposure eventually drains your energy until you are exhausted and body temperature drops significantly. When cold reaches the brain, loss of judgment occurs rapidly. The overexposed person becomes confused and may not be aware of being at unusual risk. If the dropping internal temperature is not stopped, stupor, collapse, and death will follow.

The symptoms of hypothermia are uncontrollable shivering; slow, slurred, speech; loss of hand control, memory lapses, loss of reasoning power, stumbling, drowsiness, and exhaustion.

Remember that the sufferer may deny the problem. If you see even mild symptoms, give immediate treatment. Keep the person awake and get them out of the wind, rain, and cold. Remove all wet clothing. Warm them up with warm clothes, a sleeping bag, your own body heat, and warm drinks.

Hikers, skiers, and skaters should avoid exposure by staying dry, wearing a hat, and choosing warm, waterproof clothing that covers the body and provides good protection from wind, rain, and cold. Don't drink alcohol as it causes the body to lose heat faster. Get inside if you become wet or cold.

Motion Sickness

Motion or car sickness is caused by any movement that upsets the balance control mechanisms in your middle ear. It commonly occurs when the eyes see movement that is different from what the body feels. Some people are more affected by motion than others. Motion sickness is characterized by nausea, vomiting, dizziness, and headache.

If motion sickness is a problem, medications can relieve the condition. Some of the most common are Dramamine®, Marezine®, or Bonine Wafers ®. Ask your doctor to recommend a treatment for you and the children. Make sure you know how to use them and are aware of any side effects. To be effective, you usually need to take oral medication before nausea or vomiting have started.

Car sickness may be eased by eating lightly and avoiding fried, spicy, rich, or heavy foods that can aggravate nausea.

Cut back on liquids, especially milk, before you go. Adults should avoid alcohol, cigarettes, and coffee; they can cause or worsen motion sickness. If you begin to feel nausea, sip cool water or drink ginger ale or caffeine-free cola to settle the stomach. A few dry crackers, chewing mints, or gum may help calm any queasiness.

Sufferers may benefit from loose, comfortable clothing, plenty of rest and fresh air. Open the windows—the cool air will lower the body temperature, which will help calm the stomach.

Sensitive passengers should sit in the front seat or by a window so they can see outside and directly ahead. Children should be encouraged to look forward through the windshield. Pointing out upcoming sights will help them to focus their attention on objects at a distance. A game of "Driver" may also help children. Have them pretend to steer the car with an imaginary steering wheel. Encourage them to keep their eyes on the road. Avoid calling their attention to objects at the side of the road. Other games may offer a diversion, but avoid reading, writing, coloring, or other close work.

The driver should slow down on curves and maintain a fairly constant speed. Try to avoid bumpy roads and sudden stops. Frequent rest stops for some fresh air will be appreciated by queasy travelers. Stop the car and let the victim lie down if at all possible. Encourage children to close their eyes and keep quiet and still.

Keep a sturdy plastic bag and towelettes handy in the glove compartment of the car in case someone gets sick. You can also carry a small bag of kitty litter to make any cleanup easier. Sprinkle it on to absorb the moisture and odor.

To avoid having to use the kitty litter, give a nauseous child a bag right away (even if you've only been in the car a short time or will be off winding roads in a minute). The voice of experience is speaking here!

Be calm. If you get upset, it will only make matters worse. Be sympathetic. The victim feels sick and needs your love and understanding. He is not doing it to make the trip hard for you. Be positive. Assure him that he will feel better soon and that whatever treatment you're using will work.

■ SAFETY SUGGESTIONS ■

Car Restraints

Using car seats for infants and toddlers is not only a very important safety rule, but a law in every state. Traffic accidents are a leading cause of childhood injury and death. Children are not safe sitting on a parent's lap or crawling around the car. Your chances of a serious accident are also greatly raised by the distraction caused by the movements of a baby or child while you are driving.

Buy a car seat that meets or exceeds federal safety standards. The safety of your child is worth far more than the initial cost of a good seat. You can also rent a car seat from many hospitals and community health organizations. Travelers who have left home by train or plane without a car seat can rent car seats from car rental agencies and other rental establishments.

Make sure your own car seat is easy to use. Don't buy a seat that you might not like to use. A seat that will both sit up or recline can be used for napping and sightseeing. Check to see that it fits your car and your child properly. Read the instructions carefully and make sure you use the seat correctly. If the car seat is in the back seat, put it diagonally in back of you so you can see and reach the child more easily.

Before starting the car, make sure everyone's seat belt or car seat is buckled. If you consistently use them, the kids

will accept it as routine and will not fight the rule every time. Don't allow children to share seat belts (unless absolutely necessary); do not allow them to unbuckle their restraints while the car is in motion. Wear a seat belt yourself so you are a good example to the kids.

Seat belts also help end the fight over "body space." If you can eliminate even one "she's sitting too close to me" by enforcing a family seat-belt rule, you'll be doing great!

If your children undo their seat belts, simply stop the car until the seat belts are rebuckled. A passenger who notices another not wearing a seat belt should say, "Buckle up," to that person.

Car Safety

Never leave children alone in the car. It can get very hot very quickly in a parked car. Children can die in a hot car. They can also do all kinds of damage: lock themselves in, release the car brakes. They are not safe from themselves or from strangers.

On hot days park in the shade when you can; check vinyl upholstery and metal buckles on car seats and seat belts to make sure they are not too hot. It's a good idea to cover them with a towel or blanket to protect against burning.

> To avoid catching small fingers in car doors, play "Hands Up." When you're ready to shut car doors, trunk, or hood, yell, "Hands up!" and see that everyone's hands are in the air. Then you will know that small hands are out of danger.

Avoid leaving hard, sharp, or heavy objects loose in the car. If the car stops suddenly, they can become flying missiles. Keep the dashboard and rear window ledge clear so the objects won't fly off and hit passengers or block the driver's view.

Go over the family safety rules with the children in your pretrip planning meeting. You might want to write the rules down and take them with you. Start with basics that everyone can understand. Teach the kids to keep the car doors locked and closed while traveling. Small children may try to pull on door handles if they can reach them. Forbid them to throw objects or litter out of open windows and teach them to keep heads, hands, feet, and elbows inside the car. Tell children that they may not touch the car controls, dashboard, door handles, or locks. Don't allow them to play with sharp objects in a moving car.

Explain that roughhousing, fighting, teasing, and excessive noise are dangerously distracting to the driver. Make it clear that such behavior will not be tolerated. Lastly, teach the kids to get out of the car on the side *away* from the traffic flow.

Remember never to pick up hitchhikers. Avoid heavy traffic if possible. Make frequent rest stops. If other family members drive, change drivers periodically before one becomes overtired.

Get the car serviced and roadworthy before leaving on your vacation. Make sure you have the safety equipment and emergency spare parts that you might need. Be sure to bring a duplicate key, driver's licenses for all drivers, insurance verification, and the car registration. See Chapter 1 for a complete list.

Preventing Lost Children

Before you leave home or enter an attraction, remind your children to stick together. Give them instructions on what to do if they become lost or separated from the family.

Pick out an easy-to-find meeting place. Instruct children to call for you by your first name since there are many "mamas" and "daddies."

Point out police officers and security personnel so the kids will know whom to ask for help if they get lost.

To help prevent children from getting lost, wear matching T-shirts or easy-to-spot clothing so you can be seen easily. Keep children within sight at all times. Never leave a child alone to save a place in line. Never let a child use a restroom alone.

Use a child wrist hand holder for a toddler. Available in the baby section of variety stores, this relatively new product is wonderful. It gives the child some freedom of movement to explore and run off excess energy, ensures the child won't wander off or be picked up by a stranger, and frees your hands to carry other items. It relieves a lot of stress and worry.

Count family members after a stop. This will make more sense to you if you have a large family. In crowded places, I seem to be counting constantly!

The "buddy system" works very well. Pair your family up (older children with younger) and instruct the pairs to hold hands or at least stick together. This system also helps create closer relationships among buddies. When children share the responsibility to help take care of each other and to make the outing a success, they behave better and enjoy themselves more.

Attach a whistle to each child. Teach them to use it *only* if they get lost or separated from you. These whistles give children a sense of security and are especially nice when camping.

Pin an identification tag to each child's clothing. Put it inside a pocket, jacket, or shoe so it can't be easily seen by strangers. It can be used to help locate you if the child gets lost. Include the child's name, age, parents' name and address, and the name, address, and phone number of the place you are staying. If you are going to an airport, include your airline and flight number. If going abroad, include the passport numbers.

Lost or Stolen Wallets

Before you leave home, clean out your wallet. Remove any extra cards, pictures, or papers that you won't need on your trip. Photocopy the front and back of important items such as credit cards, traveler's checks records, and your driver's license. This record will quickly tell you what was lost and pertinent information (identification numbers, telephone numbers, etc.) in case your wallet is lost or stolen. Don't keep this record in your wallet!

Take the telephone number of your bank in case your checkbook gets lost or stolen. Don't pack your money or wallet inside checked luggage.

Misplaced Car Keys

Losing the car keys or locking them in the car is a frequent worry of harried parents. *Always* have another key with you when you are traveling. It's never convenient or cheap to have a locksmith open the door or make you another key. Coat hangers can be hard to come by in a national park, and today's cars are not easily opened (unless you're a professional!).

> Give a key to another driver to carry or keep another key in your wallet or purse. I find that I might leave the keys in the ignition, but I rarely leave my purse in the car.

You can keep an extra car key hidden on the outside of the car in a small magnetic box. Don't put it under the hood if the hood has to be released from the inside. Remember where you put the key. Since that can be tricky, show and tell (uses visual and oral memory) another family member where it is hidden. Of course, don't announce it to the whole world—it's for an emergency, not for someone who wants a car in a hurry. Magnetic key holders are sold at variety or auto supply stores.

Protecting Your Car

Take some precautions when traveling by car. Keep your valuables out of sight by keeping them in the car's trunk or covered up with a blanket, pillow, or luggage. Car thieves are more likely to break in if they can see something they want.

Depending on where you are, you'll have to decide if your wallet, purse, or valuables are safer hidden in the car away from purse snatchers and pickpockets, or on your person away from car thieves. (Wasn't that an encouraging statement?)

Always lock your car each time you leave it, even if it's only for a few minutes. Don't park your car in an out-of-the-way place. Park in a well-lighted area at night. Choose a nearby landmark to help you remember where you parked. If you park during daylight hours, consider how dark or isolated the area might be if you're returning in the evening.

CHAPTER 7

Age
Characteristics
and Discipline

Age Characteristics and Discipline

This chapter is included to help you predict and cope with the general behavior of children at different ages, especially on family trips. Naturally, children will go through stages different from the generalities listed here, but certain problems and strengths are unique to each stage of development. A family vacation may be enhanced by an understanding of children's abilities and perceptions at different ages. Your children may or may not share these traits: Select those that fit and try to tailor trip discipline and activities accordingly.

Take into account and be understanding of individual differences and capabilities in children. Even within the same family children will differ in energy, moods, attention span, adaptability, and rate of development. Respect each child as an individual, and demonstrate that each child has an important place in the family.

Most children are good travelers. They are adaptable, durable, curious, energetic, friendly, funny, and enthusiastic. Capitalize on their strong points so you create good memories and build family relationships.

Remember that children do not think like adults nor see the world from an adult perspective. Give them an outlet for their energy and feelings; use their abilities and interests to make traveling exciting and interesting. Try to anticipate your children's needs and moods, dealing with them before they become a problem.

■ *CHARACTERISTICS OF AGE GROUPS* ■

The following information is provided as a guide to the probable behavior and developmental stages of children at certain ages. Tips especially suited to traveling with a child of a particular age are included to help you all enjoy your trip.

Infants

Infants are usually accommodating travelers and enjoy trips in the car. They are easier for nursing mothers who don't have to worry about fixing bottles. With all the convenience items available today (disposable diapers, ready-to-feed bottles, and wet wipes to name a few), traveling with a baby is a lot easier than it used to be.

Infants need the basics: love, food, baths, regular diaper changes, and sleep. They sleep a lot and easily, especially when the car is in motion. Best of all, they don't complain that they're bored, they don't pinch their sister, they don't wander off and get lost. Bring a new assortment of clutch toys, teethers, and rattles to keep the baby entertained.

Toddlers

Small children don't understand the concept of vacations. They might be insecure with new surroundings and situations, so be understanding. Reassure them that you'll return home and that their bed and toys will still be there. Take along a favorite cuddly toy, doll, or blanket to help comfort them.

Toddlers take each day as it comes. These children will react depending on how they feel (hungry, tired, excited), and what is happening at the moment. Toddlers get tired easily, though, and their emotions change quickly; their frustration tolerance is limited. If they can talk, they can tell you what their needs are; if not, pick up the most obvious cues and work from there. Try to figure out if they are too hot or cold, hungry, uncomfortable, or just in need of some love. A drink, a snack, a diaper change, a free run, a hug, or some combination thereof will probably do the trick.

Anxiety about strangers may now become a problem, so toddlers are happier close to familiar faces of the family. At times, however, they will attempt to be independent.

Since toddlers are mobile you can no longer put them to sleep in any convenient spot. They cope better if you can keep to their sleeping and eating schedule as much as possible. With all the newness and excitement, the same routines will provide security and comfort.

Good vacations for this age group are the informal type where you go to a destination and stay; for example, you might visit a friend or relatives, rent a cabin, go camping, or head for the beach. This enables them to keep their routine and eases the social pressure on both parent and child.

Toddlers don't have the ability to entertain themselves in a car. They love to explore, but have a short attention span for anything that does interest them. You will need to be organized to make it an enjoyable experience for them. Plan activities in advance. You might need to adjust the pace or change the type of activities frequently.

Since "no" is their favorite word, be careful to keep them positive. Issue directions in an upbeat, positive manner. This is an age of opposite extremes, yes or no. They cannot be successfully reasoned with and don't understand abstract ideas or others' needs.

You need to take control of the direction of the activities, set consistent limits, and be patient, positive, and tolerant. Give them only simple choices. Toddlers are impulsive and aggressive, but they are also sensitive. They need adult approval, praise, and love.

Preschoolers

At this age vacations are an exciting change. You will enjoy sharing their reactions and their growing awareness of our amazing world. These children have a variety of moods and boundless energy. They are curious, love new experiences and can't wait to explore.

Preschoolers are physically easier to travel with because they can talk well and do more for themselves. They don't need diaper changes or much equipment. Because of their restless energy, however, you will need to make frequent rest stops to allow them to stretch and exercise. You may have to keep daily mileage to a minimum.

They still cannot understand the meaning of time— *today* is all that matters. Still, they will show excitement for coming events.

Preschoolers ask a lot of questions and are eager learners, but have a limited understanding. They get bored easily, so have a variety of activities they can participate in to catch their interest.

This is a "we" and "me too" age. Preschoolers like to imitate and to be like others. They are good companions, friendly, affectionate, less demanding, and amusing. These children are usually easy to get along with, although they

like their own way. They can make choices and are willing
to accept suggestions. Preschoolers like to help and enjoy
new responsibilities to show they are "big."

Grade Schoolers

The family is still their main focus, their source of security
and identity, though they also need and like to be with
friends of their own age. They still accept parental authority, are loyal to the family, and are polite to adults.

Grade schoolers are generally cheerful, friendly, open
about their feelings, and optimistic. They can also be noisy,
forgetful, and restless. If they become moody, it usually
doesn't last long. These children can be judgmental and
critical of themselves and others. At the same time they are
sensitive to criticism and need parental love and approval.

They now have more self-direction and control. Listen
to their problems and be supportive. This age likes to have
responsibility, be more independent, and make some of
their own decisions. They are socially outgoing, self-
assured, practical, and eager to learn.

Grade schoolers like family activities and traveling.
They want to know about their world. They see the world
as new and exciting, full of things to do and discover.
Because of their imagination, interest, and curiosity, traveling is an exciting, educational experience for this age.

Grade school is still an age of high activity, but these
children have more stamina than younger ones. They can
tolerate more driving, but still need to have physical exercise part of the day. They are more patient than younger
siblings and can look forward to the coming activities.

Grade schoolers will be more cooperative if you allow
them to be involved in the planning of the trip and share

responsibility for its success. When deciding where to go, choose a variety of entertaining, interesting and educational places. National parks and monuments, historical sites, museums, factory tours, camping, and amusement parks are popular with this age group.

Teenagers

At this age, kids want to be with their friends more than the family. Their peer group is an important influence. Before they do something, they think about the impression it will make on their friends.

Trying to get them to do something with the family because they should is usually futile and can end in an argument. You can occasionally appeal to them "for your sake," or maybe promise them some new privilege in exchange for going on the trip.

You will need to pick activities they want to do or include their friends to get them to participate with the family. Give teens time to themselves while traveling whenever possible. They will be happier if they can have some activities with others their age away from the family.

If you have family councils, listen to your teenagers' opinions and give them a voice in the decisions. Permit them to express their ideas and feelings. Give them love, attention, and respect. You can accept and respect them as individuals without accepting all their ideas. Get in the habit of communicating with them. Talk *with* them, not at them. Try to be sympathetic and understanding of their problems and tolerant of their mood swings.

Teenagers have their own abilities and hobbies. Encourage their efforts. They also have an intelligent interest in world affairs. Share their exuberance for life by enjoying unusual and exciting adventures together.

Adolescents are self-conscious, insecure, socially oriented, complex, inconsistent, and vulnerable and strong at the same time. They have very definite ideas of what they like, but they are unpredictable; one minute they may be enthusiastic and the next they may be wishing they were home.

Teenagers can be critical, intolerant, and demanding of their younger siblings, viewing them as a nuisance and a bother. They still have affection for the family, however, even if it shows less. Remind them that exercising their right to criticize includes the responsibility to suggest practical improvements.

Occasionally teenagers will backslide toward childlike pursuits and interests. They are on an emotional roller coaster, clarifying who they are and getting used to their own feelings. As they become independent and establish individual identities, they will gradually relinquish their dependency on their parents. Teenagers are demanding new freedoms while parents are demanding new responsibilities from them.

Remember that they are in a period of rapid change. As they mature they will achieve a greater equilibrium, be happier, more responsible, appreciative, affectionate, less concerned with impressions, and more accepting of themselves and others.

Build your relationship on mutual trust, acceptance, and enjoyment. Traveling can be a natural opportunity to spend time together to strengthen relationships.

■ *DISCIPLINE WHILE TRAVELING* ■

In our vacation daydreams we sometimes think that everything will be perfect—"Shangri-La." Keep your expectations reasonable so you won't suffer unnecessary disappointment. Every moment is not going to be wonderful or exciting; days don't always work out just like you planned them. It's not realistic to expect complete harmony and perfection. If you expect it, everyone will be under a lot of pressure.

The tension and strain of being cramped up in a closed, confined vehicle is hard on everyone. Children (and parents) will become tired, hungry, bored, or just plain restless from time to time. If you can determine the reason behind the unhappiness, you can try to remedy the situation.

Sometimes the first day is the hardest, as everyone tries to settle down and adjust to being on the road.

If you have prepared well for the trip, everyone will be more comfortable and you'll cut down on frayed nerves, short tempers, arguments, hunger, boredom, and tension. We could all use less of that!

Remember to have a discussion on rules and behavior *before* your trip (see Chapter 1). Give responsibility and set reasonable behavior standards backed by appropriate discipline. Children need supervision, guidance, and consistent limits. Let your children know when you like what they're doing and when you don't. Teach them basic moral values like honesty and integrity. Be a good example in what you do and say.

It's important that parents keep their own tempers under control and handle problems in a calm, rational manner. Resist the temptation to yell or issue empty threats out of frustration. Sometimes parents threaten to "stop the car and let them walk" or "never take you anywhere ever again" if the kids don't shape up. This is not constructive and is usually counterproductive. It takes kids about two minutes (or less) to figure out that you won't really do that and that discipline is more difficult to enforce away from home.

When the going gets rough, keep your sense of humor. This will ease tension and bring problems down to size. Sometimes children can be teased out of a bad mood, but be careful you don't make the situation worse.

You need to evaluate what you are attempting to do each day of your trip. Some activities may not be feasible with children. Keep in mind that crowded, noisy attractions with long lines or strictly adult entertainment will not work with children no matter how great they are. Touring gift shops can be an unpleasant string of reprimands.

Don't demand so much that you are always giving orders. When asking children to mind you, be sure you have their attention and that your expectations are not beyond their ability.

Be adaptable if problems develop. Difficulties are bound to arise. Relax and evaluate the situation: what can be changed to make it better? Do you need to slow down because you're trying to do too much? Are you taking enough rest stops or breaks? Do you need to change direction and try a different activity? Be prepared with some possible solutions. You can either be flexible or frustrated.

If plans need to be changed, children will accept the changes and cooperate more readily if you help them understand the situation. Be sensitive to their feelings of disappointment and try to explain your decision.

Make adjustments and allowances for the different personalities of your children. One child might only need a gentle reprimand; another might need a stricter approach.

In two-parent families, both parents need to take part in taking care of and disciplining the children. Parents need to present a unified front: Discuss and agree on plans, rules, and expectations together, so children don't play one parent against the other. If you do disagree, discuss it together privately.

Sometimes the family can be handled more easily by splitting responsibilities between the parents, each taking care of certain children or duties. We find many times our children are better behaved if they are split up and taken around a museum or similar attraction in two separate groups.

■ TIPS FOR GREAT BEHAVIOR ■

The ideas related in this chapter reflect the experiences of my family and others. As you read, choose those ideas that will work with your style of parenting and your children's ages and temperaments.

The behavior, discipline, or control you have at home will continue on vacation. Children's behavior is not going to completely change because you promised if they were good you'd go to Disneyland. Don't make promises or threats you aren't prepared to carry out.

Don't expect perfect behavior all the time. Let the kids have times and places they can be themselves, run off excess energy, and don't have to be on their best behavior.

When you stop at an activity or attraction remind them of the proper behavior you expect from them. Even on vacation children need rules and consequences that are consistent, fair, and predictable. Make sure the rules fit the ages of your children and that you explain them clearly and firmly. Make sure the child understands the connection between the misbehavior and the punishment. Use logical consequences whenever possible. Give kids a warning first, but follow up with the consequence if the behavior doesn't improve. If possible, end the penalty when the behavior improves. Don't be afraid to modify rules or punishments that are too strict. Even the U.S. Constitution was amended.

> Be sure to compliment children who are behaving well. Positive reinforcement for good behavior is more effective than reprimands for poor conduct.

Children often know when they've behaved poorly. If you ignore their behavior, it may in fact worsen as the children try to get your attention. Discipline constructively by emphasizing what they can do. Keep negative comments to a minimum. Be firm but tolerant—if there are too many rules, children will only get frustrated. Children will respond more positively if the rules are reasonable and they've had a voice in making them. Children need to help regulate their own behavior.

If children are not behaving because they are overtired, nothing but rest will help. Discipline will only make the situation worse because the children can no longer cope. You might need to change your plans so the family can get some rest.

Kids in Public

Traveling often puts you in the public eye—many people feel free to approve or disapprove of your children's behavior with looks or words. I have been complimented on the beautiful manners and behavior of my "lovely" children and a few hours later received a reproachful look for the behavior of the same kids.

Parents are usually doing their best to deal with difficult situations. There have been times I've been grateful for the kind interference of a stranger who has talked with or distracted a cranky child when nothing I could do seemed to help.

Of course, you need to be considerate of other people, removing a child from a restaurant, theater, or museum if the behavior is disturbing others. Other times, well . . . how do you remove from Yellowstone Park a child who's decided to have a public tantrum? Or how should you react to an unfair remark, like the time a lady told me off because a child quietly asked me a question in a museum? In cases like these, all you can do is continue to deal with your child just as you would privately. Expect no more or less from the kids or yourself, whether people are watching or not.

I've found a lot of difference in people's tolerance of children. Although it's difficult to predict, it doesn't take long to perceive others' reactions. Are you getting smiling looks of understanding that they've been through it too? Or are you getting silent or verbal disapproval, even when you thought the kids were acting pretty good? In either case, keep calm and handle the problem as swiftly as possible with confidence and pride—even if you have to fake it.

Age Expectations

Children are basically good and want your love and approval. Be aware of the limitations and age characteristics of children. Many behaviors are the result of a stage of development. This doesn't mean you should ignore problems (unless they're minor irritations), but an understanding of your child's ability to behave well at certain ages will help you deal appropriately with misbehavior.

Toddlers: They cannot be reasoned with, nor can they learn or understand rules or foresee consequences. Correct their behavior with love and patience.

Preschoolers: These children will test the limits that are imposed. They can now be reasoned with, although they don't understand that rules apply to many situations. They are more responsive to directions and usually like to please and conform. They are often slow to obey and need to be reminded. Give them simple rules and few responsibilities. Find out why they are misbehaving and take whatever action fits the child and the situation. Young children's disobedience is largely a response to their own feelings or their perception of a new situation; it is rarely deliberate or purposeful. Correct them, but use a lot of affection, praise, and tolerance. They are motivated by the promise of a surprise or reward. Preschoolers respond well to pretending (let's walk fast like Roadrunner) or imaginative language like secret, big, strong, surprise, etc.

Grade Schoolers: Be fair and impartial in applying rules. Although they usually obey, they now question decisions, especially if you are arbitrary or inconsistent. They understand rules and consequences and how they apply. They want to be obedient, but sometimes are sidetracked and forget rules and responsibilities. Warn them in advance, remind them, and make sure they follow through. They may argue and find excuses for poor behavior, but will usually obey if consequences are consistent.

Teenagers: Try to be considerate of their needs, but give them responsibilities as well as privileges. If you are over-restrictive, they will resent it. Keep in mind that they still need and want parental attention and direction. It's natural for them to test parental authority while trying to assert themselves. Be consistent in applying rules. Avoid arguing over different points of view.

Arguments

With such close proximity, arguments are bound to arise. Try to discuss points of contention or argument ahead of time to cut down on the quarreling later.

Referee your children's arguments only when absolutely necessary (you can't allow children to physically harm one another). Otherwise you'll find yourself caught in the middle every time you try to decide whom to believe. Sometimes children will argue to gain parental attention.

Teach them to work out their problems among themselves. Their solutions can be more fair than ours since their understanding of the situation and motives are more accurate. They'll also learn how to compromise and get along with others.

It's usually best to calmly discuss problems as they occur. Identify the problem, what caused it, and possible solutions. It's important to listen to your children. Talk with them, praising their good behavior and interesting observations and listening to their points of view. This makes everyone feel good inside and motivated to do better.

Arguments can be kept to a minimum if children are not bored. Make sure you have enough activities and games to keep the kids occupied so they don't start fighting for entertainment. If you're in transit and problems arise, take the cue to stop and run off some energy.

Separating the children in a car by rotating the seating arrangements from time to time may prevent arguing. If one child is causing trouble, a parent may want to provide that individual with extra attention; sit together and chat, read a story, play a game or activity, or just snuggle for a while.

In the car, poor situations will greatly improve if a parent sits in the back. This tactic provides more control and usually separates antagonists. It's harder to pinch, poke, and fight with each other with a parent sitting right there.

Try to find ways for children to share in making the trip interesting and pleasant. Discuss how individual moods and behaviors affect the whole family. Teach children to try to be cheerful even when they are tired or the day is not going well.

If children start fighting in the car, tell them you will pull to the side of the road if the behavior continues. If they don't stop, pull over, explain the proper behavior, and stay there until they behave. Always follow through.

Children need to be purposely and directly taught to treat others with love, kindness, and respect. Take every opportunity to point out and model loving behavior. Remind them that you treat each other well and help each other because you love each other. This family philosophy will give them a feeling of security, belonging, and support.

Compliment children on loving behavior just as you would compliment completed chores.

Responsibilities

Parents need to teach children to be responsible. Every family member should have some tasks that must be completed. A group approach to chores lifts some of the burden from parents and gives the children a sense of participation and belonging. Busy children are less self-centered and less inclined to fight or quarrel. Everyone needs to help make the trip successful.

When you delegate responsibilities, make sure the person understands the job and knows how to do it. If their efforts are not sufficient, don't assume the responsibility later or do the chore yourself. Children quickly figure out how much they can get away with. You may wonder at first if the time you spend teaching and monitoring their completion is worth the effort. It is—you will get the needed help and your children will be stronger, more capable, responsible individuals.

Depending upon the nature and difficulty of each task, you might want to assign it to a specific person, rotate the responsibility, or have everyone share in helping. Prevent arguing by making sure everyone understands the schedule of responsibilities.

As you travel, delegate these jobs to the kids according to age-appropriateness: Help entertain or take care of the younger children / Bring in gear from the car / Pack the car / Help with food preparation and cleanup / Unpack the suitcases / Take care of special equipment like cameras or binoculars / Take care of personal belongings: keep them together / Empty the trash bag / Clean up the car (or room or campsite) / Make a vacation journal / Write post-cards / Take pictures / Keep financial records / Be the navigator: record mileage, routes, and destinations / Help with the driving.

Be sure to thank the children for their contributions. Praise and positive reinforcement go a long way in making kids feel good about themselves.

Rewards

Children often learn proper behavior and accept responsibility more cheerfully and quickly when their efforts are rewarded. Rewards provide positive reinforcement and motivate kids better than punishment. A reward can be as simple as your genuine appreciation and encouragement.

Parents sometimes view the vacation itself as a treat, not realizing that traveling can be difficult for children. Show your appreciation to your kids for good behavior under difficult circumstances.

The more immediately you can reinforce good behavior, the more effective the message will be. Young children in particular don't have the sense of time to understand delayed rewards. Children may stop trying if their efforts are too frustrating or seem unappreciated.

Of course, you should not reward every smile or courtesy or the completion of every task every time. After the initial learning period, your simple appreciation should be enough to give children the sense of satisfaction that comes from contributing. Children need to learn to govern their own behavior even without immediate reward. This is a lifetime process, however, and extra acknowledgment of a job well done rarely has a negative effect.

CHAPTER 8

Activities

Activities

To entertain your children you'll want to take some toys and plan some activities that your children can enjoy on your vacation. They'll be happier and so will you if you pack up some old favorites and a few new surprises for the whole family.

Children love to play with their parents, but be careful that you don't dominate or take over their play. Of course, you can't entertain your children all the time. Sometimes they need to play by themselves, read, or take a nap. When you first start out, the excitement of leaving will be enough in itself for a while.

A vacation is the perfect time for families to talk together. Reminisce about exciting or happy experiences. Tell family stories and history. Kids love to hear about their parents' courtship and marriage; their parents' childhoods; family struggles involving courage and decision; tales of relatives they know or may not have met yet.

Discuss current events with your older children. Read aloud the travel brochures about the trip. While you have a captive audience you can discuss family goals and activities. And, of course, play games and sing songs together.

■ *TOYS AND TOTES* ■

When choosing toys to take along select compact, lightweight, versatile items that will provide the most play value and variety in a small space. Don't take anything that can be broken or swallowed. Remember that things get lost easily while traveling, so don't take items that are small, expensive, or have a lot of pieces. Leave behind messy materials or projects or items that require special care.

To make sure the kids (and the toys) will be safe if the car stops suddenly, don't take any hard, sharp objects. Avoid toys that will distract the driver. A noisy toy will quickly drive you crazy in the enclosed confines of a vehicle!

You might want to rotate the selection of toys in the passenger area to avoid clutter and maintain the kids' interest. Keep some of them in the trunk so your children don't get tired of them all at once. Save a few new toys for a hard day or the latter part of the trip.

Children will be better about keeping tidy if they each have a special place for their toys and activities and a litter bag to dispose of wastepaper. Set some guidelines on what the kids can take. Let them be responsible for taking care of and carrying their own toys.

Make a rule to use one toy at a time, putting it away before getting out another. If the children find that rule difficult to follow, you might want to keep the toy bag and pass out toys one at a time.

Keep the child's toys and books within easy reach. If you have two children in car seats, fill a diaper bag or tote with toys they can easily reach on the seat between them.

You can use backpacks, zipper bags, or athletic bags to hold toys, books, and souvenirs. A drawstring bag can be hung from the clothes hook in the back seat of the car. You can also give kids a cardboard box for storing their things; use a flat box that will slide under the front seat when not in use.

A lunch box can be a good container for small toys, markers, notepads, mini-puzzles, etc. Use a different color box for each child. A flannelboard can be made by gluing felt to one side. Magnetic letters and numbers will stick to it if it's metal. (Don't forget to pack the flannel pieces and letters.)

You can make a lap tray by covering a small suitcase with a cloth, using a lap-style TV tray, or bringing a clipboard. My favorite to use is a 9-by-11-inch cake pan with a metal sliding lid. The lid can be used as a hard work surface, and toys and souvenirs can be put inside the pan. Avoid plastic lids: They pop off and they break easily.

An activity kit can be made out of a three-ring binder and resealable plastic zip-type bags. With the openings at the top, punch three holes on the left side of the bags and reinforce them. Then add art supplies, small toys, etc. This idea is better for older kids since it requires organizing skills to keep it neat.

Over-the-seat car organizer pockets are nice to hang on the back of the front seat. You can make one to fit your car. Use a yard and a half of heavy material. Add two bands of $1^1/_2$-inch-wide elastic at the top and bottom ends and slip these loops around the seat; attach pockets to fit your needs. Use the pockets to hold toys, books, shoes the kids have taken off, sunglasses, maps, tourist information, tissues, first aid kit, flashlight, wet wipes, snacks, baby bottles, diapers, and writing supplies.

■ *ACTIVITY IDEAS* ■

Let the children choose a few favorite toys from home for the trip. Pack some new toys and books to surprise the kids and keep up their interest level. I like to put away a few familiar toys well before the trip, so that they seem more interesting.

A large variety of items are suitable for trips, but don't take them all or there will be too much to keep track of and not enough room in the car for the people! The following section includes ideas for children of a broad range of ages. (Ideas for infants, toddlers, and older children follow these basics.)

■ storybooks

■ cassette player with story and sing-along tapes, music tapes, earphones, and extra batteries

■ magazines, both current (to read) and old (to cut out pictures and make a collage or a "wish" book of toys, games, or books)

■ a favorite songbook

■ books with riddles, quizzes, puzzles, brain teasers, word and number games, magic tricks

■ workbooks with dot-to-dot, mazes, math, pencil games, hidden pictures and words, crossword puzzles

■ comic books

■ note pads or tablets of colored paper and drawing and writing paper

■ sticker books, coloring books

■ school assignments

■ pens, pencils, colored markers or pencils, and crayons

■ (Be careful of the heat with crayons—they melt. I bring only eight crayons so there aren't so many to keep track of. Watch your child carefully with markers—some kids like to decorate their bodies instead of the paper. Definitely buy washable markers.)

■ miscellaneous equipment like an eraser, a ruler, a pencil sharpener

■ blunt safety scissors

■ tape, a glue stick (least messy option), and a stapler

For crafts, games, and imaginative play, choose:

■ modeling clay (avoid the sticky kind)

■ sewing cards (you can make your own out of old cards)

■ pipe cleaners (twist into shapes and people)

■ card games (Old Maid, Snap, Animal Rummy, Fish, War, Crazy Eights, Concentration, or Memory)

■ flash cards

■ miniature toys (soldiers, cars, airplanes, trains, cowboys, Indians, doll furniture, animals, and space creatures)

■ small toys such as those found in cereal boxes or novelty stores and most typically used as birthday party prizes or stocking stuffers

- large snap-together blocks or a small construction set

- magnets, compass

- puzzles in frames

- kaleidoscope

- Etch-a-Sketch®

- magnetic alphabet board

- blackboard with chalk

- Magic Slate® (picture disappears when you lift the cellophane—great for tic-tac-toe, hangman, etc.)

- Colorform® stickers (for car windows)

- paper bags to make puppets, masks, hats, etc.

- flannelboard with flannel pictures

- hand or finger puppets

- paper dolls

- favorite stuffed toy (tie an elastic loop around the toy's neck so it can be carried on a wrist, stroller handle, etc.)

- small doll with clothing

- doctor or nurse kit

- play telephone

- hand-held electronic video games

- magnetic games such as bingo, chess, and checkers

- small pinball games

Babies need special toys of their own. I like to tie toys to the child's car seat so they can't be lost easily. This is especially handy when they're in that lovely stage of throwing their toys. Nearly all babies will be entertained by some combination of these tried-and-true toys and games:

- plastic, cloth, and cardboard books

- teethers

- plastic keys, rings, measuring spoons

- soft stuffed toys

- squeak toys

- cloth ball

- mirror

- blocks

- rattles

- pinwheel

- Play games that involve finding a hidden object, tracking sound identification, and favorites such as peek-a-boo, pat-a-cake, and This Little Piggy.

Small children love:

- books

- stories

- songs

- rhymes

- fingerplays

- puppets

- dolls

- stuffed animals

- simple games

- They also enjoy using their imaginations. Because they have short attention spans, be prepared with a wide variety of activities and games. Make up games that use music, make-believe, picture identification, body parts and object identification, and other learning activities that involve recognizing the way things feel, taste, smell, sound, look, go together, and are different.

Older children don't need as many structured activities since they can help entertain themselves and the smaller children. They can even stand some boredom. Older kids should be well entertained with these supplies:

■ radio with earphones

■ travel journal or vacation scrapbook

■ inexpensive camera

■ crafts such as knitting, crocheting, or embroidery

■ *Guinness Book of World Records* (This is interesting, entertaining, and good for making up games.)

■ Older kids often enjoy map-reading and may like to help you plan routes if you are traveling by car.

If your children are happily occupied, leave well enough alone. When they become bored, introduce new or favorite activities to help entertain them. Some of these games and activities may become family traditions, adding to your memories of enjoyable trips.

Surprise Packages: Wrap up snacks or new small toys in tissue paper, foil, comic pages, or odd pieces of wrapping paper. Use lots of string and tape. These can be opened on difficult occasions such as a delay at an airport or a day with a long drive, or they can be used as prizes for counting so many trucks or telephone booths or as rewards for particularly good behavior. A present, no matter how trivial, is always exciting, and the kids look forward to the surprises. Save a few packages for the trip home.

> *Car Fairy:* Kids love make-believe. You might want to adopt a "car fairy" who mysteriously leaves small presents, good traveler awards, or notes expressing love or promising "special happenings." The fairy comes while children are napping or are away from the car.

Special Occasions: If you're on the road on a birthday or holiday, make a special effort to celebrate the occasion. The kids will remember the event for years to come. You can purchase special paperware to eat on, favors, candles, cupcakes, and ice cream. Give a birthday child small gifts, special privileges, or even a speech in his or her honor. If a gift is to be given upon returning home, present the child with a gift certificate for later redemption.

Ice-Cream Eating Contest: Buy a carton of ice cream and have an ice-cream eating contest. A carton (or two) is less expensive than a visit to an ice-cream parlor and the contest atmosphere nearly ensures that you will use up all you bought. It's fun for the whole family and everyone will remember eating all the ice cream they wanted.

Purse: Keep a play purse in the car with a wallet or coin purse, play money, coupons, comb, small mirror, play or old jewelry and compact, keys, toy car, small doll, lip gloss, etc. This collection should be kept for car use only, so the child doesn't get tired of it. Even on short trips, it will always be there and ready to go.

Grab Bag: Keep a tote bag containing toys for use in the car, at grandparents, a doctor's waiting room, or elsewhere. Change the toys periodically so the kids don't get bored.

Collections: Take some containers for children to make nature or trip collections. Shoe boxes, baby food jars, plastic margarine tubs, plastic medicine bottles, resealable zip-type plastic bags, paper sacks, and envelopes are good for this activity. Bring along some labels, a magnifying glass, and reference books such as *Golden Nature Guides*, *Audubon Society Beginner's Guides*, and *Eyewitness Books*.

Vacation Collection: Take a large manila envelope for each child to collect trip mementos. Kids often like to save brochures, postcards, and hotel stationery.

Vacation Scrapbook: Buy a self-stick photo album your child can use to make a scrapbook out of souvenirs, brochures, tickets, menus, postcards, pictures, stickers, artwork, and other items collected on the trip. A scrapbook will keep a child busy and will provide a lasting memento. Magnetic albums are great because they can be made as you travel. They don't require glue or corners, and the items can be rearranged.

Travel Journal: A notebook can be used as a journal or diary of your trip. Drawing pads can be used by smaller children to draw pictures of what they've seen and done. They can draw and write a record of daily happenings such as where they went, what they saw and did, memories, impressions, weather, the people, and food. Children can make their own diaries, or you can have a family journal with everyone making entries. This record is a personal keepsake that is likely to outlast an inexpensive souvenir.

Postcards: Buy postcards to remember what you saw on your trip. Write on the back what you did that day. This gives you a pictorial record and journal of your trip. The postcards can be arranged in an album as you travel or when you arrive home.

Photo Album: If you have an instant camera, take along a self-stick photo album to mount and label pictures along the way. You could appoint an older child "Trip Photographer" or "Photographer of the Day."

Sticker Book: Kids love stickers and they can collect bumper stickers, state stickers, attraction stickers, and novelty stickers. Let them put them on plastic or self-stick photo album pages.

Picture Book: Let the children make a book of their favorite pictures by cutting pictures out of magazines and pasting them in a notebook. They can also make an alphabet book by cutting out a large letter for each page (in alphabetical order), and a variety of pictures to paste on each page.

Logbook: Older children can keep track of information about the trip and passengers. For example, they can record departure and arrival dates, times, who went, odometer readings; home port, destination, places you've seen, sights you've visited, important events, points to remember for the next trip, distance traveled, journey time, weather, costs, gas used, gas mileage (divide the distance traveled by the amount of gas used), and the average speed (divide distance travelled by the time you have been in transit).

Map Reader: Mark your route on a map. Let a child keep track of your progress, marking the distance you've covered. This gives children a sense of time and distance and answers the "When will we get there?" question.

Make a Map: To help children gain a sense of space and distance, have them draw a map of their neighborhood. It should show their house, friends' houses, streets, schools, and any landmarks.

Navigator: Older children usually enjoy studying maps and brochures. They can help plan routes, watch for road signs, parking spaces, keep you on course, read about points of interest, keep records of your route and journey, gas purchases, mileage, and trip expenses.

Happiness Is: Family members take turns telling what happiness means to them. For example, "Happiness is going to Grandma's," "Happiness is eating ice cream," "Happiness is a loving family."

Silly Rules: Make up silly rules for the car. For example, lift your feet when you go over a bridge; duck your head when you go under a bridge; and when you go through a tunnel raise your hands, close your eyes, and make a wish!

Imagination: Look at the passing scenery and try to spot shapes like objects, animals, or faces in the clouds, trees, rocks, buildings, lakes, rivers, and other scenery.

Creative Drawing: Take lots of paper for making pictures. Have the kids draw pictures of what they see on your trip.

Scribbles: Draw a large letter, a scribble, or the child's initials on a piece of paper. Let the child create a picture, animal, face, or silly object out of it. This is a great imagination activity, even for toddlers.

Mad Monsters: Give each passenger a piece of paper and have them fold it into thirds. Decide on a category like animals, birds, or people (or all three). Each person draws a head. Players then fold the papers so that their drawings cannot be seen except for the tips of the lines at the bottom. The papers are then traded, and the middle or body is drawn connecting the drawing with the top lines. When the second drawing is finished, fold the paper again and pass it to someone else. This person finishes the feet or bottom of the picture. When you're finished, look at the mad monsters you've created!

Finger Tracing: Trace letters, numbers, facial parts, shapes, or other objects on a child's back. Let the child try to guess what you made, then "erase" it and start again.

Finger Messages: Trace letters on someone's palm to make a short message. After understanding the letter given, the child briefly closes the palm and opens it again for the next letter.

Who's There?: Pick out an interesting house or car, and ask "Who's There?" The children use their powers of observation and imagination to describe the inside of the house or car, who is in it, what they look like, how they spend their time, their likes, dislikes, favorite foods, pets, careers, wealth, happiness, etc. This game is especially entertaining when the players make up the reasons for the details of the story.

This Place: When you go to a new town or city ask questions about it to get your children to observe and think. Ask, for example: How old is the town? Where did it get its name? What are the businesses or industries that support it? Who lives here? Are they wealthy or poor? Are they happy? Do they like their town?

What If?: Discuss what to do in difficult, dangerous, or happy situations. For example: What if you were offered candy by a stranger? What if you got lost? What if you could eat whatever you wanted? What if you could be anything, anywhere, or anybody in the whole world? What if you were the parent, what would you do? What if you could spend the day however you wanted, what would you do?

Learn Skills: This can be a good opportunity to teach children their address, phone number, the alphabet, or counting. They also practice skills such as whistling, writing their names, tying shoes, telling time, memorizing a rhyme, etc. Older children can memorize poems or learn

Morse code, the deaf alphabet, knot-tying, paper folding, magic tricks, and more. To make it entertaining, you can pretend to be a news reporter and "interview" your child, asking and reviewing questions. Just don't overdo it or it may become a drill.

Traveling Show: Plan a show that you put on during the trip. Let each person share a talent or skill (maybe a just-learned one—see previous activity). You can have a puppet show, stories and poems, magic tricks, jokes, etc. This activity is especially enjoyable in a motel after you've settled in for the night.

Talk-Show Host: Using a tape recorder, let someone document the trip events, interview the other passengers about what has impressed them on the trip, tell funny stories, sing, or interview someone who pretends to be a famous historical character from the area that you're visiting.

Puppets: Make hand and finger puppets and use them to tell stories and sing songs. They can be easily made by drawing facial features on paper bags. Stick puppets can be made by gluing a picture of a face or small figure on a popsicle stick. You can have ten actors by drawing tiny faces on your fingertips with washable felt-tip pens.

Puzzles: Bring puzzles in frames or make your own. Use a picture from a calendar or a postcard or use one the child has drawn. Tear it up in a number of pieces according to the skill of the child.

■ *STORIES* ■

Children love to be read to and traveling gives you the time and opportunity you often lack at home. Listening to a story is soothing, relaxing, and educational. Wondering what will happen next draws the family together, and you will all remember wonderful stories instead of long, tedious miles or boring stopovers. Read favorite stories from your childhood or ask your librarian, bookseller, or children's teachers for suggestions on the best books for your children's ages and interests. *The Read Aloud Handbook* by Jim Trelease and *The New York Times Parent's Guide to the Best Books for Children* by Eden Ross Lipson are excellent resources for oral reading choices.

Some of our family's favorite books are:

Homer Price, by Robert McCloskey
Ramona Quimby, Age 8, by Beverly Cleary
Henry Huggins, by Beverly Cleary
Mr. Popper's Penquins, by Richard and Florence Atwater
The Velveteen Rabbit, by Margery Williams
Cheaper by the Dozen, by Frank Gilbreth
Little House on the Prairie, by Laura Ingalls Wilder
Charlotte's Web, by E.B. White
James and the Giant Peach, by Roald Dahl
Where the Wild Things Are, by Maurice Sendak

Other suggested favorites are:

Young Readers 3-6
The Maggie B., by Irene Haas
Make Way For Ducklings, by Robert McCloskey
Brave Irene, by William Steig

What Do You Do with A Kangaroo? by Mercer Mayer
If You Give A Mouse A Cookie, by Laura Joffe Numeroff
Where the Sidewalk Ends, by Shel Silverstein

Grades 1-4
The Littles, by John Peterson
The Indian in the Cupboard, by Lynne Reid Banks
Owls in the Family, by Farley Mowat
The Courage of Sarah Noble, by Alice Dalgliesh

Grades 3-7
Sarah, Plain and Tall, by Patricia MacLachlan
The Pond, by Robert Murphy
The Search for Delicious, by Natalie Babbitt
Where the Red Fern Grows, by Wilson Rawls
If I were in Charge of the World and Other Worries, by Judith
  Viorst
The Incredible Journey, by Sheila Burnford
The Lion, the Witch and the Wardrobe, by C.S. Lewis
Rascal, by Sterling North
Tuck Everlasting, by Natalie Babbitt

If you prefer to listen, or if reading in the car makes you ill, many excellent stories are available on audiocassettes from your library or bookstore. You can play them in your car player if you have one or bring along a portable battery-operated player.

Audiocassettes
Just So Stories, by Rudyard Kipling
The Adventures of Tom Sawyer, by Mark Twain

The Musicians of Bremen, by Anderson
The Call of the Wild, by Jack London
Ring of Bright Water, by Gavin Maxwell
Winnie the Pooh, by A.A. Milne
The Snow Goose, by Paul Gallico
The Red Badge of Courage, by Stephen Crane
Through the Looking Glass, by Lewis Carroll
The Wind in the Willows, by Kenneth Grahame

Flannelboard Stories: You can make a flannelboard by gluing felt to the inside of a box lid; store the figures in the box. You can also place the figures on a towel hanging over the back seat. The easiest way to make figures, letters, and numbers is to buy Pellon at a fabric store, draw the pictures on the Pellon with crayons and markers, and cut out. Kids love to make up and tell flannelboard stories.

Continuing Story: Someone starts to tell a story, either make-believe or based on an actual event or circumstance experienced on the trip. There should be one or more characters, a setting, and a problem. Encourage details in the stories. The more absurd the subject, the more fun it is! After a few sentences or minutes, the storyteller stops at an exciting part and says, "And then." The next person then continues the story, starting where the previous person left off. Continue as long as you want until the story reaches an exciting conclusion or becomes hopelessly boggled! This is a terrific way to use your imagination and creativity. Avoid scary or sad stories for young children.

Street Story: Each person takes a turn making up part of a funny story using words seen on signs along the road. For example: "I was walking down 'quality' street, met

'George' whom 'you can trust,' and ate 'ice cream' in a 'pet store.' And then . . . (Another player continues the story.)"

Tall Tales: Give each person a piece of paper and tell them to "fan fold" it into eight sections. A fill-in-the-blanks story sequence is explained to all players. Each person then starts by writing a funny name on the second section, folding the top so the name is concealed, and passing it to someone else. Then everyone writes something to fit the next part of the sequence, folds it again, passes it, and so on. The sequence is: (name) went to _____ and met _____. They said _____ and decided to go to _____ but, on the way _____, so they decided to _____. When you are finished, unfold the papers and read them out loud using the sequence to make funny sentence stories.

Family Tales: While you're all so close together, create a family poem or song! Have someone write down the ideas so you don't forget them while you're working on it.

CHAPTER 9

Games

Games

Children and adults of all ages love to play games. Games are a great way to interact as a family. They keep a child's attention, pass the time, and also create fond memories. A child's age, attention span, and interests will determine your child's favorite games and how often you will need to go on to a new game.

Vary the difficulty of the games to a child's age and ability. You will be surprised both at how fast younger children understand the games and at the power of a simple game to entertain even older children. You can determine the length of play in many games by a certain time period or number of miles. You can also create teams; for example, in a car the front seat passengers can play against the back seat passengers.

Play games with younger children in a slow, simple way so they can enjoy them. Don't be too strict about enforcing the rules—they often cannot understand the concept fixed rules. Try to play as a group instead of competing—young children care more about the sheer joy of participating than winning. The competitiveness will only frustrate them, especially if someone else always wins. Children over the age of five are able to deal with rules (and winning and losing) much better.

If you are traveling by car, don't let the games become so noisy or boisterous that they distract the driver. The driver might be able to participate in some of the simple games, but he or she should concentrate on the driving.

Many of the games can be played by or adapted for one person. There are also variations listed so you can adapt them to the needs or desires of your children. Preparation for some of the games is easier to do at home, but it is possible to do all preparation on the road. In most cases, no special items are needed. A few games will need a pencil, an eraser, a note pad to keep score, typing paper, graph paper, dice, a dictionary, and/or a watch for timing.

■ *CATEGORY LISTS* ■

The following lists include categories of ideas and objects to use in playing many of the games. These lists will give you a wide variety of choices to make each game enjoyable and different.

General: animals, birds, fish, automobiles, vehicles, transportation, cities, states, countries, flowers, plants, toys, food, beverages, candy, colors, books, stories, television shows, movies, songs, male or female names, cartoon characters, storybook characters, Bible characters, movie stars, television personalities, sports figures or teams, political figures, friends, relatives, neighbors, hobbies, buildings, signs, landmarks, vacation words, camping equipment

Animals: horse, cow, pig, sheep, deer, squirrel, chipmunk, snake, skunk, cat, dog, chicken, duck, goose, birds, animal drinking water or eating, lying down, on left or right side of road, in truck or trailer, tied up, black and white animal, white, grey, or red animal, with horns, scratching itself, dogs in other cars

Vehicles: bulldozer, tractor, dump truck, road equipment, tow truck, semi truck, oil or gas truck, garbage truck, refrigerator truck, mail truck/jeep, bus, taxi, motorcycle, recreational vehicle, truck and camper, sailboat, speed boat, police car, fire engine, bicycle, ambulance, farm machinery, foreign car, convertible, moving van, jeep, station wagon, van, Volkswagen Beetle

Cars and Trucks: same color as yours, white, black, red, or two-toned, pulling a boat, house trailer, horse trailer, towing another vehicle, only one headlight, flashing lights, rooftop carrier, trailer hitch, a flat tire, visible spare tire, hood open, door open, with lettering, making a left or right turn

Transportation: airplane, bus, helicopter, train, boat or ship, roller skates, bicycle, trolley or streetcar, cable car

Buildings: gas station, fire station, post office, pet store, library, florist, barn, church, school, castle, mansion, supermarket, home, log cabin, movie theater, drive-in theater, lighthouse, motel, hotel, restaurant, drugstore, mobile home, with fire damage, ice cream store, car dealer, with a two-color roof, red or blue roof, colored, round, with a broken window, under construction, brick building, metal building, government building

People: police officer, firefighter, mail carrier, road worker, person riding a horse, train engineer, bus driver, food server, ballplayer, cook or chef, lifeguard, farmer, golfer, swimmer, boater, taxi driver, bellhop, porter, bicyclist

Signs: yield, stop, speed limit, slippery when wet, hospital, school crossing, railroad crossing, cattle crossing, crosswalk, merge, no U turn, no left turn, no right turn, do not enter, keep to the right, one-way, reduce speed, no parking, stoplight, for sale, no vacancy, the word *zone*; round sign, sign indicating distance, sign on a tree, sign with vertical or diagonal lettering, sign with an arrow, U.S. on it, information sign

On the Road: bridge, dirt road, cloverleaf, freeway on ramp, tunnel, tollbooth, railroad crossing, beginning drivers in a marked car, license plate of a particular state

By the Road: golf course, playground, farm, cemetery, junkyard, pine tree, any tree, fire hydrant, statue, park bench, barber pole, weather vane, U.S. flag, ladder, haystack, awning, telephone booth, mailbox, trash can, crane, windmill, water tower, windsurfer, lawnmower, kite, white picket fence, swing set, street lamp, hubcaps, dislodged mufflers, airfield or airport, flowers, garage sale, billboard

Water: pond, lake, reservoir, river, waterfall, fountain, swimming pool, ocean, bay, creek, stream

Thirteen Colonies: Delaware, Pennsylvania, Rhode Island, North Carolina, South Carolina, Virginia, New York, New Hampshire, Maryland, Connecticut, Georgia, New Jersey, Massachusetts

United States Presidents:

1. George Washington
2. John Adams
3. Thomas Jefferson
4. James Madison
5. James Monroe
6. John Quincy Adams
7. Andrew Jackson
8. Martin Van Buren
9. William H. Harrison
10. John Tyler
11. James K. Polk
12. Zachary Taylor
13. Millard Fillmore
14. Franklin Pierce
15. James Buchanan
16. Abraham Lincoln
17. Andrew Johnson
18. Ulysses S. Grant
19. Rutherford B. Hayes
20. James A. Garfield
21. Chester A. Arthur
22. Grover Cleveland
23. Benjamin Harrison
24. Grover Cleveland
25. William McKinley
26. Theodore Roosevelt
27. William H. Taft
28. Woodrow Wilson
29. Warren G. Harding
30. Calvin Coolidge

31. Herbert C. Hoover
32. Franklin D. Roosevelt
33. Harry S. Truman
34. Dwight D. Eisenhower
35. John F. Kennedy
36. Lyndon B. Johnson
37. Richard M. Nixon
38. Gerald R. Ford
39. James E. Carter
40. Ronald W. Reagan
41. George Bush

Fifty States and Capitals

Alabama - Montgomery
Alaska - Juneau
Arizona - Phoenix
Arkansas - Little Rock
California - Sacramento
Colorado - Denver
Connecticut - Hartford
Delaware - Dover
Florida - Tallahassee
Georgia - Atlanta
Hawaii - Honolulu
Idaho - Boise
Illinois - Springfield
Indiana - Indianapolis
Iowa - Des Moines
Kansas - Topeka
Kentucky - Frankfort
Louisiana - Baton Rouge
Maine - Augusta
Maryland - Annapolis
Massachusetts - Boston
Michigan - Lansing
Minnesota - St. Paul
Mississippi - Jackson
Missouri - Jefferson City
Montana - Helena
Nebraska - Lincoln
Nevada - Carson City
New Hampshire - Concord
New Jersey - Trenton

New Mexico - Santa Fe
New York - Albany
North Carolina - Raleigh
North Dakota - Bismarck
Ohio - Columbus
Oklahoma - Oklahoma City
Oregon - Salem
Pennsylvania - Harrisburg
Rhode Island - Providence
South Carolina - Columbia
South Dakota - Pierre
Tennessee - Nashville
Texas - Austin
Utah - Salt Lake City
Vermont - Montpelier
Virginia - Richmond
Washington - Olympia
Wisconsin - Madison
West Virginia- Charleston
Wyoming - Cheyenne

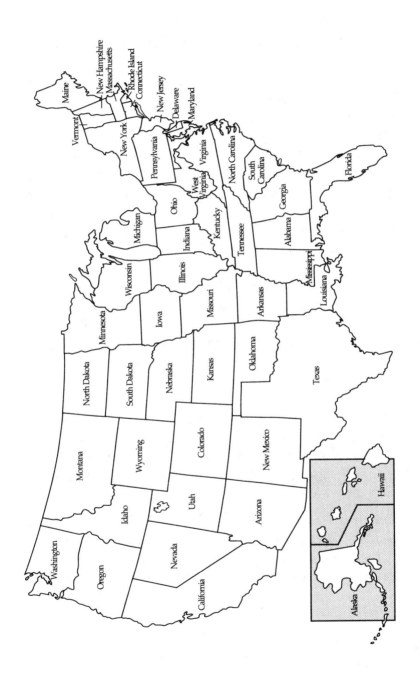

■ *LICENSE PLATE GAMES* ■

It just wouldn't seem like a road trip without playing at least one of these classics.

Map: Using a map of the United States (you may copy the one in this book), see how many of the states you can find on license plates; color in each state on the map as you find it. This game works especially well on longer trips and helps teach children geography. To make the game harder, use the map without any names on it, filling in the name of the state also.

Get That Number: Each player chooses a number from zero to nine and tries to find that number on license plates. Score one point each time a player spots the number, three points if it's found twice on the same plate, and five points if it's found three times. The first person to get twenty points is the winner.

Word Search: Each player thinks of a word or phrase that contains eight letters and tries to find the letters to spell their word or phrase first. Each letter has to be found in order on signs or license plates. The first player to complete the word or phrase wins.

Variations: Choose a word such as a child's name, the place you are visiting or heading toward, a favorite food, etc., for all the players to use. Use simple words like car, toy, or dog for smaller children.

Bingo: Use bingo cards and have someone call off the first one or two digits on license plates for the players to mark off on their cards. The first player to cross off five numbers in a row horizontally, vertically, or diagonally calls out, "Bingo!" and is the winner.

Variation: You can make bingo cards that have twenty-five squares with states' names written in them. As players spot a license plate from a state on their cards, they mark off that square.

Foreigner: Players look for out-of-state license plates. The first player to spot one calls, "Foreigner," and receives one point. The first player to recognize the state calls its name and receives a point. Another point is received for naming the capital of the state or province.

■ *OBSERVATION GAMES* ■

These games can last a long time and are more enjoyable if they are not played on freeways, where there's not so much to see.

Try to focus the search on objects that you are likely to see on that particular day or in a particular place; otherwise this game becomes frustrating, especially for small children. Include a couple of unusual or fun objects in each game.

Alphabet: Players look for letters of the alphabet in their proper sequence on roadside signs and license plates. The first one to complete the alphabet wins. Players can agree to use a certain side of the road or set a time limit; players can divide into teams and can call out the letters as they see them or play the game quietly.

Variation: Small children can look for numbers one through nine.

Travel Bingo: Make up bingo cards with twenty-five squares: five across and five down, with the center left as a free space. Draw a picture or write the name of an object in each square. Each column can have a different category or type of object (road signs, buildings, animals, vehicles, state license plates, etc.), or they can be arranged randomly. Each card can be different, or the same items can be arranged on all the cards in different orders. Play the game just as you would play Bingo: Cross off each object as it is found. The first one to complete five in a row in any direction is the winner. For a long trip, you can play "Blackout," in which all the spaces must be found. If you don't want to make your own set, this game is available at many toy and drugstores.

Treasure Hunt: Give each child a different list of commonly seen objects. Include hard and easy items on each list as fairly as you can. When a player sees an object he or she calls out its name and checks it off the list. The first player to cross off all the items on the list calls out, "Treasure," and is the winner.

Variations: Give each child the same list of objects; the first one to call out an object gets to claim it. Or you can give one point for each item found. The player with the most points at an agreed-upon time limit is the winner.

Bumble: Each player chooses a different color of car. Players say, "Bumble," when they see a car of their color. Give each player one point for each "Bumble." The first player to get twenty points is the winner.

Car Snap: Choose a make of car that is easily identified—for example, a jeep, a station wagon, a van, etc. The first person to spot that type of car calls out, "Snap," and receives a point. No one else can claim it. If "Snap" is incorrectly called, the player loses a point. The player with the most points at an agreed-upon time is the winner.

Automobile: One player can challenge another to identify the make and model of a car within view. If the player guesses correctly, a point is earned; if the player is wrong, a point is lost. A player with a score of minus ten is out of the game. The challenger has to identify the car if the opponent cannot. If the challenger also fails, a point is taken from his or her score. Be sure to pick cars you can see long enough to verify the make and model.

How Many?: Choose familiar objects such as a gas station or telephone booth found on the road. Each player guesses how many will be seen within the next five minutes. Count them along the way, and have someone watch the time. The player to guess closest to the correct number is the winner.

Guess: Each player guesses how many traffic lights in ten the car will go through without having to stop. The one with the closest guess is the winner.

Number Cruncher: Each player looks out one side of the car and tries to find as many numbers as possible, mentally adding each digit together (zeros don't count, of course). The first player to reach one hundred is the winner.

I Spy: One player thinks of an object that is inside or outside the vehicle (If the object is outside, players must look and guess fast!). The principal player then says, "I spy with my eye something _____ outside (or inside) the car." The other players try to guess the object spied. The spy can give clues such as the color, size, number of letters, or the first initial of the object, but should not give the answer away by looking at the object. Answer guesses with a yes or no. The first player to guess the object correctly calls out "I spy _____." He or she is the winner and gets to pick the next item to spy. If no one guesses corectly, the spy gets another chance to stump the other players.

Hide and Seek: Each player takes a turn pretending to be an object in the car. The other players ask questions to try to determine the "identity" of the principal player. If help is needed, the principal player can give clues like "cold" or "freezing" if far away, or "warm" or "hot" if close. Older children might want to be parts of the car such as a fender to make the game more difficult.

Desert Island: A player starts by saying, "I would need a _____ (names a visible object) on my desert island because _____." The next player continues the phrase, listing the object already mentioned and adding a new object and the reason it's needed on their desert island. Players are out of the game if they forget an object or can't complete the reason. The last player left in the game is the winner.

Suitcase: Each player chooses ten objects to take on vacation and writes them on a list. The players then try to find objects on the trip that begin with the same letter and are the same color as the objects on their lists. For example, to be able to take a blue radio, you can find a blue river. When you find a match, call "suitcase" so the other players can make sure it's correct. The first player to "pack" all the items on a list is the winner.

Graveyard: Choose an object or category (i.e., animals, people, buildings, vehicles, etc.) for the players to count or find objects in. Set a winning score or time limit. Each player or team uses only one side of the road. Each time the object is spotted a point is received. If the object crosses the road, the first player or team to call it gets it. If a white horse is spotted, double your score. A point is lost if a player makes a false claim. If you get a graveyard on your side of the road, you have to bury your cows, etc., and start over.

Zoo: Each player collects animals for a zoo. You get to capture the animal for your zoo if you are the first to spot it and call out its name. If you call out the wrong animal name, it escapes and can be captured by someone else. The player to capture the most animals is the winner.

Mileage: Choose an object that can be seen in the distance. Players (except driver!) close their eyes and say "Now" when they think your car is passing it. The closest one wins.

Variations: Each player guesses how many miles and/or minutes it will take to reach the object or place. Or, pick a starting point and have the players guess the miles traveled until you say "stop." Players can also close their eyes and guess the speed of the car. Appoint one passenger the odometer-, speedometer-, and/or clock-watcher to see which player is the closest.

Slogans: Read the top line on billboards and signs. Make up a second line that is related to the first and rhymes with it. For example, to "Eat Here" you can add "For Cheer."

■ *WORD GAMES* ■

Twenty Questions: A player chooses a person, place, or thing for the other players to identify. The player indicates the category. To make the game easier, you can also give the object's location. For example: "I'm thinking of a thing in the _____" (toy box, refrigerator, yard, etc.). The players take turns asking up to a total of twenty questions that can be answered with a "Yes" or "No." Remember that a guess counts as a question. The player to guess correctly chooses the next object. If no one guesses, the player who chose is the winner and takes another turn.

Variation: A player chooses an object and describes it to the other players as an animal, a vegetable, or a mineral. You can also keep score, adding up the number of questions or guesses used to correctly guess the object. Add that number to the score of the player who chose the object. The one with the most points at the end of the entire game is the winner.

Who Am I? One player is selected to close his eyes and cover his ears while the others decide who or what the player will be. They may choose a Bible figure, movie star, sports figure, cartoon character, storybook character, television character, political figure, friend, relative, neighbor, animal, etc. The player then asks questions to find out the identity of the character. For example, "Am I real, a person, animal, on television, in a story, liked, famous, alive, etc.?" The player is allowed three guesses to his identity. Choose a limit to questions of five minutes, five miles, or up to twenty questions. Decide on the limit before you begin to play.

Dictionary: Each player takes a turn picking a word from the dictionary and giving a definition (either correct or false). The other players try to guess if the definition is correct. If they are fooled, the principal player gets five points. If they guess correctly, the principal player loses five points. The player with the most points at the end of play is the winner.

Banana: A player chooses a verb (describe this to younger players as a word that shows action, such as run, play, or jump). The other players try to guess the verb by asking up to ten questions, changing the verb in the question to the word "banana." For example, "Do you banana at home? Have I banana'd today? Am I bananaing right now?" Only one direct guess is allowed to each player. The players earn five points each time they guess correctly.

Straight Face: Choose someone to be "it" and direct that player to answer questions from the other players with a silly phrase such as "a monkey's tail, sausages, or pink toads." The task of the principal player is to answer every question with a silly phrase—without smiling or laughing. For example: "What do you eat with ice cream? What's your favorite toy? What do you comb your hair with?" The person to make the player laugh is the next "it." Change the silly phrase frequently for best results.

Link Up: A player starts by saying the name of a country, state, city, county, mountain, river, body of water, continent, island, desert, etc. The next player says another geographical location that starts with the last letter in the first player's word, and so on. For example, if Wyoming were used, the next player would start with a word that begins with G like Georgia. No location can be used more than once. You are out of the game when you can't think of a word. The last player left wins. Hint: Think of a lot of A words ahead of time. If you want to make the game more challenging, use fewer categories, limiting answers to countries and lakes, for instance.

Variation: Go through the alphabet in sequence naming locations for each letter. You can also play this game with categories like animals or foods.

Categories: One player selects a category to be used. (The general category list on pages 179-183 has lots of good ideas.) Each player then takes a turn naming something in that category within an allotted time limit. A name can only be used once, so you might want to keep a written list of what's been used. If players can't think of a word, they are out of the game. The last player left wins! To make the game harder, make the categories more specific. For example, instead of animals, use only dogs.

Going on a Trip: A player starts by saying "I'm going on a trip, and I'm taking a _____ (object that starts with the letter *A*, like apple)." The next player continues the game, repeating what the first player said and adding a *B* word. The next player repeats what the first two said, adding a *C* word and so on through the alphabet. The game is especially amusing when silly items like a song, Aunt Tilly, a toothbrush, a cold, a Frisbee, or ants are taken on the trip. Players are eliminated when they forget something or can't think of a word to add. The last player left is the winner.

I Went to the Store: A player starts this game by saying, "I went to the store and bought a _____ (word beginning with *A*, like apple or avocado)." The next player repeats the previous words and adds a *B* word like biscuit or beverage. Players are eliminated if they forget the previous words. The last player left is the winner.

Variation: If you forget your grocery list, buy anything you want on each turn instead of items in alphabetical order. Players may recall items in any order.

Grandfather's Store: A player starts this game by saying, "I went to Grandfather's Store and bought something _____" (give a clue such as color, size, or taste). The other players then take turns asking questions about the purchase that can be answered with a "yes," "no," or "maybe." For example, "Is it large?" "Can you eat it?" "Is it sweet?" The first player to guess correctly gets to go to "Grandfather's Store" and make the next purchase. If the purchase isn't guessed, the player who made the purchase gets to buy another item.

In the Attic: A player starts this game by saying, "In the attic there's an ____ ____ (anxious ape or any other two words that begin with *A*)." The next player starts the sentence in the same way, "In the attic there's a ____ ____," but adds two *B* words like "brave bat," and so on through the alphabet. Players are given a point if they use words that don't start with the correct letter, or if they cannot think of anything to say in time to keep the rhythm of the game going. The player with the fewest points is the winner. This game can also be played without keeping score.

Alphabet Traveling: This game starts with the first player choosing a destination, a way of getting there, and a reason for going. Begin with the letter *A*. For example: "I'm going to Alabama on an alligator to attack ants." The next player uses a phrase with *B* words. Continue this game in sequence through the alphabet. If a player can't think of an alphabet phrase, he or she is out of the game. The last player left wins. This game can also be played without keeping score.

Variation: You can use a different dialogue and add an alphabetical name, for example, "I'm Aaron, I come from Alaska, and I like apples."

I'm Traveling: A player starts this game by choosing a state or country and giving clues until someone guesses the state or country. For example: "I am the state known for my potatoes." Answer: Idaho. "I have a famous clock called Big Ben." Answer: England. The player who guesses correctly chooses the next place.

Grandma's Cat: In this game you see how ridiculously you can describe "grandma's cat." A player starts by saying "Grandma's cat is an ____(adorable or awkward) cat." The next player adds a descriptive word that begins with B, saying for example, "Grandma's cat is an adorable, bald cat," and so on through the alphabet.

Ghost: This is a challenging game for older children. The first player thinks of a word with four or more letters and says the first letter of that word. The next player adds another letter in sequence that could make a word (each player must have a specific word in mind). Then the next player also adds a letter to the others, and so on. The object is to add letters *without* completing a word. If you name a letter that completes a word or cannot think of a word, you get a letter G. The next time you get an H, and so on. If you complete the word "ghost," you "disappear" from the game. If you can't think of a word, you can bluff and say a logical letter, or you can forfeit your turn and receive a "ghost" letter. When you add a letter to the word in play, another player may challenge whether you are really thinking of a legitimate word. (Challenges are only allowed immediately after a new letter is added.) If you have a word you must say it out loud, and the challenger gets a letter from "ghost." If you are bluffing, you get the letter from "ghost." After such a challenge, you start another round. The last player left in the game is the winner. Remember that the word can change each time someone adds a letter. Try not to end words or you won't have a "ghost" of a chance!

Variation: Instead of spelling the word "ghost," the first time someone completes a word he or she becomes a "half ghost." The next time, the player becomes a complete ghost and "disappears" from the game. Anyone who talks to a ghost becomes a half ghost the first time and a complete ghost the second time, "disappearing" also. The ghosts can try to draw others into talking with them.

Word Associations: A player starts by calling out a word. The next player quickly says another word that is brought to mind by the first word. The next player immediately says a word that calls to mind the new word, and so on. A player can be challenged and receives a point if the others agree a word doesn't have a legitimate connection. The player with the fewest points is the winner.

Double Words: The first player uses a word pair like daylight. The next player uses another compound word that begins with the last word of the preceding pair, i.e., lighthouse, and so on. Try to continue the game as long as you can.

Teakettle: A player secretly chooses a pair or set of homonyms (words that sound alike, but have different spellings or meanings); for example, *pain* and *pane*, may be chosen. The player then gives sentences with the word replaced by "teakettle," such as "Did you wash the window teakettle?" or "I have a teakettle in my arm." The other players try to guess the teakettle word. The player who guesses the word chooses the next homonyms.

Forbidden Word: In this conversation game, the family decides on a word that must not be spoken like "yes," "no," or "I." Then, as you are talking or asking questions, try to trick the others into saying the forbidden word. A player who says the word receives a point. The player with the fewest points is the winner. To make the game harder, pick several forbidden words.

Buzz: Players count aloud in turn from one to one hundred, but without saying the number seven. Players must say "Buzz" every time a number has a seven in it (i.e., seven, seventeen, twenty-seven) or is a multiple of seven (i.e., fourteen, twenty-one, twenty-eight). When seventy is reached the players say "buzz one, buzz two," and so on. A player who forgets to say buzz appropriately is out of the game. The last one left is the winner.

Variation: To make it harder, add another word substitute such as "Fizz" for the number five. Say "Fizz" every time you reach a number with five or a multiple of five in it. For example, fifty-seven will be "Fizz-buzz."

Capital Cities: A leader calls out the name of a capital city. The first player to name the city's state gets a point. The player with the most points wins.

Variation: Name the state and see who can name the capital city.

Name the State: Using a map, name three to four cities or towns in a certain state. See if the kids can name the state.

United States: Have the players try to name the fifty states, the state capitals, the presidents, the original thirteen colonies, a state and its bordering state, or other U.S. trivia. Give points for each correct answer.

State Neighbors: You'll need a United States map for this game. The first player says "I am California," and the other players quickly name the states that border California. The player to name the most bordering states becomes the next state. Players may pretend to be any state in any order.

What Do You Know About Me? Each player in turn asks the others questions like "What is my favorite food (or color, game, television show, sport, school subject, holiday, song, book, friend, hobby, or activity)?" The first player to answer the question correctly gets a point. Several players can be called on for the correct answer. If no one can answer correctly, the principal player can tell the others the answer. The player with the most points is the winner. This game can also be played just for fun without scoring.

Family Trivia: A player asks a trivia question relating to the family. For example: What is your cousin's name who lives in Boston? Who loves the Beach Boys? The player who guesses correctly asks the next question. If no one guesses the answer, the first player can ask another question.

I'm Thinking of Someone: A player describes another person in a positive way (through an admirable character trait, a special or unusual activity, or a notable accomplishment, etc.). The player should start by giving vague clues, becoming more specific as the game continues. Avoid revealing the sex of the person—speak of them as "this person." The other players try to guess who is being described. Each player can guess only once so guess carefully. If you are the one being described, you may not guess yourself. The player to guess correctly gets to describe the next person. Continue the game until everyone has been described at least once. This is a great opportunity to make everyone feel special.

■ *PENCIL & PAPER GAMES* ■

Travel: Give every player a piece of paper and tell them to print the word travel vertically in the left margin. Using the initial letters of *travel*, each player writes down as many words associated with travel as begin with those initial letters; for example, train, truck, and tunnel or railway, road, and roam. The player who thinks of the most words within a specific time period is the winner.

Variation: Use the word *geography* and write down geographical locations (countries, states, cities, rivers, lakes, oceans, etc.).

Hidden Words: Print a long word such as *explorations, automobiles, vacation,* or a city or state of your destination. Players should write down words made from the letters in the original word. A letter can only be used the same number of times it is used originally. The player with the most bona fide words at the end of a certain time period or distance limit is the winner. Simple words are acceptable for young children; older children should try to form more difficult words.

Scramble: Scramble some trip-related words (cities, states, national monuments, attractions, etc.). See who can unscramble them first.

Famous Partners: At the word "Go!" players list frequently paired words on a piece of paper. For example, they may write "coat and hat," "rain or shine," "salt and pepper." The player with the most pairs is the winner.

Variation: For young children, give half of a combination and see if they can provide the missing half.

Hangman: This is a game for two players. One player thinks of a word, draws a gallows on a piece of paper and draws the correct number of blank lines under the gallows to correspond to the number of letters in the word. Before beginning to play, the players agree to the number of guesses that will be allowed (equal to the parts of the hanged man). If the guesser names a correct letter, the letter is written in the correct space. (If a letter occurs twice or

202

more in the word, fill in all the places that it appears.) If the guesses are incorrect, they are written on the page (so players remember what has been guessed), and a part of the hanged man is made. Usually the figure has a circular head, a line for a body, and four lines representing two arms and two legs, making a total of six guesses. You can add shoes, hands, and facial features if desired. If a player guesses the word before the figure is finished, he or she is given a point and the opportunity to be the hangman for the next word.

Spelling Bee: A parent chooses words from newspapers, magazines, and books that are appropriate for the children's ages. Each child spells a word in turn, receiving a point for each correctly spelled word. The player with the most points at the end of a time or distance limit is the winner. Even if a player misspells, he or she stays in the game. This game can also be played in teams; incorrectly spelled words are given to the opposition, which must spell it and a new word correctly.

Tic-tac-toe: This old favorite is great on trips. Play it on a Magic Slate® (lift the plastic film to erase the slate) if you have one. Make two lines horizontally and two lines vertically so that they intersect to make nine spaces. One player is X, and the other is O. Each player takes a turn making their symbol in a square. The first one to get three of their symbols in a row going in any direction is the winner. Take turns being first each game, since the first player has an advantage. If no one wins, it's a "cat's eye."

Variation: Play tic-tac-toe in reverse by trying to force the opponent into a "losing" combination of three in a row.

S.O.X.: This is a harder version of tic-tac-toe. For this game make a larger grid with three lines each way for a total of sixteen squares. Add another player whose mark is *S*. The first move by each player must be made in an outside square. After the first move, the game is played like tic-tac-toe. The first player to put three of their symbols in a row is the winner.

Battleship: This is a game for two players. Each player uses a gameboard drawn on a piece of graph paper. Using markers or crayons to make a heavy line, box in ten spaces across and ten spaces down (one hundred squares per box). Number 1 through 10 down one side of each grid, one number to each square; write A through J across the tops to reference the spaces. Give one gameboard to each player. On the bottom grid, each player positions his or hers own ships; the top grid is used to record the "shots" made at the opponent. Each player secretly places his or hers own ships by coloring in squares to represent each ship. A battleship requires four squares; a cruiser needs three squares; and the two destroyers take two squares each. After each player has positioned the ships, the players take turns calling out one shot at each turn using letter-number coordinates such as "B-5." Each player records the shots and hits by shading in the squares for misses and marking with an X for hits. If an opponent hits a space with a ship, the ship is sunk. The hit player then must say, "You hit my _____." The first player to sink the opponent's four ships is the winner.

Variation: To make the game harder (and larger), require that all the spaces a ship occupies are "hit" to sink it. Make 400 (20x20) squares, marking 1 through 20 down, and A through T across. Mark one battleship (five squares); one cruiser (four squares); two destroyers (three squares each); and two submarines (two squares each). Instead of alternating shots, each player gets the same number of shots at each turn as the number of ships still afloat. After all shots in a turn have fired, the player is told what ship is hit, but not which shot hit it. This adds some mystery and difficulty to the strategies.

Connections: On a piece of paper, make a square grid of rows of dots, any size. Each player draws a vertical or horizontal line to connect two adjoining dots. Try to avoid connecting the third side of a box to keep the other players from completing a box. If a line that is drawn makes a complete box, that player puts his or her initial in the box, then takes another turn either drawing a line, or completing a box. The player's turn ends when he or she cannot close a box. When all potential boxes have been made, the player with the most boxes initialed is the winner.

Snakes: This game is played like connections except the players may add only to the end of the previous connection, making one long snake. No diagonal lines or skipping spaces is allowed. The winner is the last player to draw a line without connecting the snake.

Match the Sets: Each player takes a sheet of paper, and randomly writes the letters of the alphabet (or numbers 1 through 25) all over. Leave some space around each letter and circle each one. Then write the letters again, scattering them all over the paper far from the duplicate letters. The papers are now passed to another player. The first player to connect all the sets with a line from one letter to its match without crossing or touching any other lines is the winner.

Quizzes: Prepare quizzes on a variety of topics like animals, history, and geography. For example, list foods and ask which animals eat them; ask for the male and female names of animals; list animal babies and ask for the name of each one's mother; ask for the sounds of particular animals; ask for the home or habitat of particular animals; list customs or features of nations and ask which country it is. Gear this game to the children's ages. When the children complete the quizzes, give a point for each correct answer.

Variation: You can make the quizzes multiple choice by listing some answers to choose from.

Crossword Puzzles: Older children sometimes like to make their own crossword puzzles. The words and clues can be centered on the trip.

■ *LIMITED ACTION GAMES* ■

Follow the Leader: This car version starts with a passenger doing a simple motion. The next person repeats it, adds a motion, and so on. For example: Clap hands, wiggle nose, scratch arm, shake hands, cross your legs, rub your face, etc. Players who forget a motion or don't give it in the correct order are out of the game. The last player left is the winner.

Simon Says: This game can be adapted by using motions like those in "Follow the Leader." The leader (Simon) quickly gives a command. If it is preceded by the phrase "Simon says," the players obey. If it is not, the players must ignore the command. If Simon gives one command and does another, obey the command Simon says. Players are out of the game if they obey a command that Simon didn't give. The last player left is the winner and plays "Simon" for the next game.

Concentration: Agree on a category from which to choose words (cars, vacation words, animals, flowers, fruits, road signs, states, etc.). This is a rhythm game that begins when all players, in unison, slap their knees twice, clap their hands twice, snap their fingers, then repeat. Each player must call out a word when the fingers are snapped or be out of the game. A player is also out if he or she repeats a word already used. Make the game more challenging by stepping up the rhythm a little each time. The winner is the last one left.

Variation: When the fingers snap, one player can say the name of another player. On the next snap of the fingers, the player named gives the name of someone else, and so on. A player who misses the rhythm or says the name of someone not present is "out."

Rock, Scissors, Paper: This old game is loved by children. The players hide their hands behind their backs and form their hands to represent a rock, scissors, or paper. Rock is the hand in a fist, scissors is the middle and index finger formed in a v-shape like a pair of scissors, and paper is the palm down, hand flat. Then they say together, "Rock, scissors, paper." As they finish saying "paper," they quickly put their hands in front of them. Each object beats another. If the hands all open the same, it is a draw. Paper covers a rock, rock can break scissors, and scissors cut paper. You can keep score or play just for fun.

■ *QUIET GAMES* ■

SSHHHH: Everyone tries to remain quiet for as long as possible (parents too!). The last one to speak is the winner.

Variation: Those players who speak or make noise are out of the game but then try to get the others to talk.

Speechless: Players do not speak for a certain length of time or until a specific object is spotted along the road. During this time players communicate with written signs and body language.

Whisper: Have everyone whisper for a certain mileage or time period. You can give points to anyone who forgets and speaks out loud. The player with the fewest points is the winner.

Make Me Laugh: One player is "it" and tries to make the others laugh during a certain time or distance limit. The principal player is allowed to make funny faces but cannot make any noises (no humming, talking, whispering, singing, etc.). Whoever laughs first becomes "it."

Charades: Decide on a category to be used such as animals, movies, books, songs, etc. Use simple actions like eating or brushing teeth for small children. Each player takes a turn by silently acting out a word or short phrase for the others to guess. No questions can be asked; only guesses can be made. The first player to guess correctly is the winner and the next performer.

Lifesaver: This is an old favorite of our family. Even the driver can play this! Give each person a Lifesaver® and see who can make it last the longest! You'll get a lot of mileage out of one sweet and a nice respite from the wagging tongues.

■ *WAITING GAMES* ■

To help pass the time while waiting in a place where loud activity would disturb others, try these fun games.

Waiting Room: Have someone time you to see how long it takes you to spot the people listed. Try to beat your time the next time! You can also make up your own list.

1. A man wearing a hat
2. A woman pushing a stroller
3. A girl wearing white shoes
4. A baby sucking on a pacifier
5. A woman reading a newspaper
6. A boy wearing an orange or red jacket
7. A man carrying a briefcase
8. A girl eating candy
9. A baby crying
10. A boy chewing gum

What Can You See?: If you are waiting somewhere, ask your children to look around and find items of a particular shape, size, texture, or color. For example, find all the objects that are square, hard, little, red, etc. Talk about how objects can be both different and alike.

Take a Trip: One player pretends to be the conductor. The other players sit in a row and pretend they are travelers on a trip. The trip takes six stops to get to the final destination. The conductor starts the game by holding both closed hands out to the first passenger, with a small object (the ticket) hidden in one hand. The conductor asks the passenger which hand holds the ticket. If the traveler guesses correctly, he or she moves forward one space (stop). Each traveler gets a turn to guess which hand holds the ticket. Passengers who do not guess correctly stay in their seats, but when they finally move forward for a correct guess, any subsequent wrong guesses require that they move back one space to "look" for their ticket. The first traveler to reach the final sixth stop is the winner and becomes the next conductor.

Critter: The object of this game is to be the first player to complete your critter bug. Each player takes turns rolling the dice to collect the parts for a critter to be drawn on a sheet of paper. Number one gets a body, number two a head, number three a leg, number four an eye, number five an antenna, and number six a tail. A critter has one body, one head, six legs, two eyes, two antennas, and one tail. Draw each critter part as you collect it. The first player with a complete critter is the winner.

CHAPTER 10

Songs and
Fingerplays

Songs and Fingerplays

Singing is an enjoyable entertainment as well as a terrific way to expend energy and relieve boredom while traveling. Some of the best memories you'll create on your vacation will be singing as a family. This chapter includes the words to favorite songs and fingerplays. Now you don't need to remember all the words and verses to be able to sing! You also might want to bring along songbooks and tapes such as the Wee Sing series, *Traffic Tunes* by Joe Scruggs, *Car Tunes* by Stephen Elkins, or Vicki Lansky's *Sing Along as You Ride Along*. You can enjoy these classic tunes as they are written or use a familiar tune and make up new lyrics about your family or vacation. You also might want to play "Name That Tune." Have someone hum, clap, or whistle a tune. The first person to guess the name of the song is the winner and chooses the next song. In addition, many of the songs can be performed in a round. *Row, Row, Row Your Boat* is a favorite.

■ SONGS ■

ARE YOU SLEEPING

Frère Jacques, Frère Jacques
Dormez-vous? Dormez-vous?
Sonnez les matines, Sonnez les matines
Ding, Dang, Dong! Ding, Dang, Dong!

Are you sleeping? Are you sleeping?
Brother John, Brother John
Morning bells are ringing, morning bells are ringing
Ding, Ding, Dong, Ding, Ding, Dong!

(This song is often sung as a round.)

THE BEAR WENT OVER THE MOUNTAIN

The bear went over the mountain
The bear went over the mountain
The bear went over the mountain
To see what he could see.

The bear went over the mountain
The bear went over the mountain
The bear went over the mountain
And what do you think he saw?

The other side of the mountain
The other side of the mountain
The other side of the mountain
And what do you think he saw?

Grass on the side of the mountain
Grass on the side of the mountain
Grass on the side of the mountain
And what do you think he saw?

A tree in the grass on the mountain
A tree in the grass on the mountain
A tree in the grass on the mountain
And what do you think he saw?

A nest in the tree on the mountain
A nest in the tree on the mountain
A nest in the tree on the mountain
And what do you think he saw?

A bird in the nest on the mountain
A bird in the nest on the mountain
A bird in the nest on the mountain
And what do you think he saw?

A flea on the bird on the mountain
A flea on the bird on the mountain
A flea on the bird on the mountain
And what do you think he saw?

An eye on the flea on the mountain
An eye on the flea on the mountain
An eye on the flea on the mountain
And that is what he saw!

BINGO

There was a farmer had a dog,
And Bingo was his name,
B-I-N-G-O,
B-I-N-G-O,
B-I-N-G-O,
and Bingo was his name, Oh!

There was a farmer had a dog,
And Bingo was his name,
(Clap) I-N-G-O,
(Clap) I-N-G-O,
(Clap) I-N-G-O,
and Bingo was his name, Oh!

There was a farmer had a dog,
And Bingo was his name,
(Clap, clap) N-G-O,
(Clap, clap) N-G-O,
(Clap, clap) N-G-O,
and Bingo was his name, Oh!

There was a farmer had a dog,
And Bingo was his name,
(Clap, clap, clap) G-O,
(Clap, clap, clap) G-O,
(Clap, clap, clap) G-O,
and Bingo was his name, Oh!

There was a farmer had a dog,
And Bingo was his name,
(Clap, clap, clap, clap) O,
(Clap, clap, clap, clap) O,
(Clap, clap, clap, clap) O,
and Bingo was his name, Oh!

There was a farmer had a dog,
And Bingo was his name,
(Clap, clap, clap, clap, clap),
(Clap, clap, clap, clap, clap),
(Clap, clap, clap, clap, clap),
and Bingo was his name, Oh!

The farmer's dog's at our back door,
Beggin' for a bone
B-I-N-G-O,
B-I-N-G-O,
B-I-N-G-O,
And Bingo was his name! Oh!

CLEMENTINE

In a cavern, in a canyon,
Excavating for a mine,
Dwelt a miner forty-niner,
And his daughter Clementine.
Chorus

Light she was, and like a fairy,
And her shoes were number nine,
Herring boxes without topses,
Sandals were for Clementine.
Chorus

Drove she ducklings to the water
Every morning just at nine,
Hit her foot against a splinter,
Fell into the foaming brine.
Chorus

Ruby lips above the water
Blowing bubbles soft and fine;
As for me, I was no swimmer
And I lost my Clementine.
Chorus

How I missed her, how I missed her,
How I missed my Clementine,
Then I kissed her little sister,
And forgot dear Clementine.
Chorus

Chorus
Oh, my darling,
Oh, my darling,
Oh, my darling Clementine!
You are lost and gone forever,
Dreadful sorry, Clementine!

THE FARMER IN THE DELL

The farmer in the dell,
The farmer in the dell,
Heigh-ho, the derry-o,
The farmer in the dell.

The farmer takes a wife,
The farmer takes a wife,
Heigh-ho, the derry-o,
The farmer takes a wife.

The wife takes a child,
The wife takes a child,
Heigh-ho, the derry-o,
The wife takes a child.

The child takes a nurse,
The child takes a nurse,
Heigh-ho, the derry-o,
The child takes a nurse.

The nurse takes a dog,
The nurse takes a dog,
Heigh-ho, the derry-o,
The nurse takes a dog.

The dog takes a cat,
The dog takes a cat,
Heigh-ho, the derry-o,
The dog takes a cat.

The cat takes a rat,
The cat takes a rat,
Heigh-ho, the derry-o,
The cat takes a rat.

The rat takes a cheese,
The rat takes a cheese,
Heigh-ho, the derry-o,
The rat takes a cheese.

The cheese stands alone,
The cheese stands alone,
Heigh-ho, the derry-o,
The cheese stands alone.

FIVE LITTLE MONKEYS

Five little monkeys jumping on the bed,
One fell off and bumped his head.
Mama called the doctor and the doctor said,
"No more monkeys jumping on the bed!"

Four little monkeys jumping on the bed,
One fell off and bumped his head.
Mama called the doctor and the doctor said,
"No more monkeys jumping on the bed!"

Three little monkeys jumping on the bed,
One fell off and bumped his head.
Mama called the doctor and the doctor said,
"No more monkeys jumping on the bed!"

Two little monkeys jumping on the bed,
One fell off and bumped his head.
Mama called the doctor and the doctor said,
"No more monkeys jumping on the bed!"

One little monkey jumping on the bed,
He fell off and bumped his head.
Mama called the doctor and the doctor said,
"No more monkeys jumping on the bed!"

No more monkeys jumping on the bed.
No more monkeys bumping their head.
No more calling doctors and doctors no more said,
"No more monkeys jumping on the bed!"

FOUND A PEANUT

(Sing to the tune of *Clementine*)

Found a peanut, found a peanut
Found a peanut just now
Just now I found a peanut
Found a peanut just now.

Cracked it open, cracked it open
Cracked it open just now
Just now I cracked it open
Cracked it open just now.

It was rotten, it was rotten
It was rotten just now
Just now it was rotten
It was rotten just now.

Ate it anyway, ate it anyway
Ate it anyway just now
Just now I ate it anyway
Ate it anyway just now.

Got a stomachache, got a stomachache
Got a stomachache just now
Just now I got a stomachache
Got a stomachache just now.

Called a doctor, called a doctor
Called a doctor just now
Just now I called a doctor
Called a doctor just now.

Died anyway, died anyway
Died anyway just now

Just now I died anyway
Died anyway just now.

Went to heaven, went to heaven
Went to heaven just now
Just now I went to heaven
Went to heaven just now.

Met St. Peter, met St. Peter
Met St. Peter just now
Just now I met St. Peter
Met St. Peter just now.

Ate a peanut, ate a peanut
Ate a peanut just now
Just now I ate a peanut
Ate a peanut just now.

GRAND OLE DUKE OF YORK

The Grand Ole Duke of York
He had ten thousand men
He marched them up the hill
He marched them down again
And when you're up you're up
And when you're down you're down
And when you're only halfway up
You're neither up nor down!

(Repeat three times getting faster and faster each time.)

HOME ON THE RANGE

Oh, give me a home, where the buffalo roam,
Where the deer and the antelope play;
Where seldom is heard a discouraging word,
And the skies are not cloudy all day.
Chorus

How often at night when the heavens are bright,
With the lights from the glittering stars;
Have I stood there amazed and asked as I gazed
If their glory exceeds that of ours.
Chorus

Where the air is so pure and the zephyrs so free,
The breezes so balmy and light
That I would not exchange my home on the range
For all of the cities so bright.
Chorus

Chorus
Home, home on the range,
Where the deer and the antelope play,
Where seldom is heard a discouraging word,
And the skies are not cloudy all day.

I HAD A LITTLE BROTHER

I had a little brother,
His name was Tiny Tim
I put him in the bathtub,
To teach him how to swim.

He drank up all the water,
He ate up all the soap,
He tried to eat the bathtub,
But it wouldn't go down his throat.

I called the doctor,
I called the nurse;
Who called the lady
With the alligator purse?

"Mumps" said the doctor,
"Measles" said the nurse,
Nothing said the lady,
With the alligator purse.

Then out went the doctor,
Out went the nurse,
I paid the lady
With the alligator purse.

I KNOW AN OLD LADY

I know an old lady who swallowed a fly,
Now I don't know why she swallowed a fly,
Perhaps she'll die.

I know an old lady who swallowed a spider,
That wriggled and jiggled and tickled inside her.
She swallowed the spider to catch the fly,
Now I don't know why she swallowed a fly,
Perhaps she'll die.

I know an old lady who swallowed a bird,
Now, how absurd to swallow a bird!
She swallowed the bird to catch the spider,
That wriggled and jiggled and tickled inside her,
She swallowed the spider to catch the fly,
Now I don't know why she swallowed a fly,
Perhaps she'll die.

I know an old lady who swallowed a cat,
Now imagine that, to swallow a cat!
She swallowed the cat to catch the bird,
She swallowed the bird to catch the spider,
That wiggled and jiggled and tickled inside her,
She swallowed the spider to catch the fly,
Now I don't know why she swallowed a fly,
Perhaps she'll die.

I know an old lady who swallowed a dog,
What a hog to swallow a dog!
She swallowed the dog to catch the cat,
She swallowed the cat to catch the bird,
She swallowed the bird to catch the spider,
That wiggled and jiggled and tickled inside her,
She swallowed the spider to catch the fly,
Now I don't know why she swallowed a fly,
Perhaps she'll die.

I know an old lady who swallowed a cow,
I don't know how she swallowed a cow.
She swallowed the cow to catch the dog,
She swallowed the dog to catch the cat,
She swallowed the cat to catch the bird,
She swallowed the bird to catch the spider,
That wiggled and jiggled and tickled inside her,
She swallowed the spider to catch the fly,
Now I don't know why she swallowed a fly,
Perhaps she'll die.

I know an old lady who swallowed a horse,
. . . She died, of course!

IF YOU'RE HAPPY AND YOU KNOW IT

If you're happy and you know it
Clap your hands (clap, clap)
If you're happy and you know it
Clap your hands (clap, clap)
If you're happy and you know it
Then your face will surely show it
If you're happy and you know it
Clap your hands (clap, clap).

If you're angry and you know it
Stamp your feet (stamp, stamp)
If you're angry and you know it
Stamp your feet (stamp, stamp)
If you're angry and you know it
Then your face will surely show it
If you're angry and you know it
Stamp your feet (Stamp, Stamp).

If you're sad and you know it
Shed a tear (sniff, sniff)
If you're sad and you know it
Shed a tear (sniff, sniff)
If you're sad and you know
Then your face will surely show it
If you're sad and you know it
Shed a tear (sniff, sniff).

If you're tired and you know it
Make a yawn (ahhhh)

If you're tired and you know it
Make a yawn (ahhhh)
If you're tired and you know it
Then your face will surely show it
If you're tired and you know it
Make a yawn (ahhhh).

If you're happy and you know it
Sing a song (la la la)
If you're happy and you know it
Sing a song (la la la)
If you're happy and you know it
Then your face will surely show it
If you're happy and you know it
Sing a song (la la la).

(You can make up many verses to this, or just repeat the "If you're happy and you know it" verse with the following variations:

Whistle a tune
Snap your fingers
Nod your head
Click your tongue
Tap your toes
Roll your eyes
Knock your knees
Click your heels)

IT TAKES A WORRIED MAN

It takes a worried man
To sing a worried song.
It takes a worried man
To sing a worried song.
It takes a worried man
To sing a worried song.
I'm worried now
But I'm not gonna worry long.

It takes a happy man
To sing a happy song.
It takes a happy man
To sing a happy song.
It takes a happy man
To sing a happy song.
I'm happy now
And I'll be happy all day long.

It takes a loving man
To sing a loving song.
It takes a loving man
To sing a loving song.
It takes a loving man
To sing a loving song.
I'm loving now
And I'll be loving all along.

I'VE BEEN WORKING ON THE RAILROAD

I've been working on the railroad
All the live-long day.
I've been working on the railroad
Just to pass the time away.

Don't you hear the whistle blowin'?
Rise up so early in the morn.
Don't you hear the Captain shoutin',
"Dinah, blow your horn!"

Dinah, won't you blow,
Dinah, won't you blow,
Dinah, won't you blow your horn?
Dinah, won't you blow,
Dinah, won't you blow,
Dinah, won't you blow your horn?

Someone's in the kitchen with Dinah
Someone's in the kitchen I know.
Someone's in the kitchen with Dinah
Strummin' on the old banjo.

Fee-fie-fiddle-ee-i-o,
Fee-fie-fiddle-ee-i-o,
Fee-fie-fiddle-ee-i-o,
Strummin' on the old banjo.

JOHN JACOB JINGLE HEIMER SCHMIDT

John Jacob Jingle Heimer Schmidt
That's my name, too.
Whenever I go out the people always shout
There goes John Jacob Jingle Heimer Schmidt!
Da-da-da-da-da-da-da.

(Repeat this verse four times, each time becoming softer until on the last verse you're only whispering the lines. End by singing da-da-da-da-da-da-da very loud.)

LITTLE SKUNK

Well, I stuck my head in a little skunk's hole,
And the little skunk said, Well bless my soul,
Take it out! Take it out! Take it out!
Remove it!

Well, I didn't take it out,
And the little skunk said,
If you don't take it out, you'll wish you had,
Take it out! Take it out! Take it out!
Remove it!

(Pinch nose) Psssssss
TOO LATE!

MAKE NEW FRIENDS

Make new friends,
But keep the old,
One is silver,
And the other gold.

A circle's round,
It has no end.
That's how long
I want to be your friend.

(This is a good song to sing in rounds.)

MICHAEL FINNEGAN

There was an old man named Mich-ael Fin-ne-gan,
He had whiskers on his chin-e-gan.
The wind blew them off and they grew in-a-gain.
Poor old Mich-ael Fin-ne-gan be-gin a-gain.

There was an old man named Mich-ael Fin-ne-gan,
He went fish-in with a pin-a-gain,
Caught a fish but dropped it in-a-gain.
Poor old Mich-ael Fin-ne-gan be-gin a-gain.

There was an old man named Mich-ael Fin-ne-gan,
Climbed a tree and scraped his shin-a-gain,
Took off sev-eral yards of skin-a-gain,
Poor old Mich-ael Fin-ne-gan be-gin a-gain.

There was an old man named Mich-ael Fin-ne-gan,
He grew fat and then grew thin-a-gain,
Then he died and had to be-gin a-gain.
Poor old Mich-ael Fin-ne-gan be-gin a-gain.

THE MORE WE GET TOGETHER

(Sung to tune of *Did You Ever See A Lassie*)

The more we get together,
Together, together,
The more we get together,
The happier we'll be.

For your friends are my friends,
And my friends are your friends,
The more we get together,
The happier we'll be.

OH, SUSANNA!

I come from Alabama
With my banjo on my knee,
I'm going to Louisiana,
My true love for to see.
Chorus

It rained all day the night I left,
The weather it was dry,
The sun so hot I froze to death,
Susanna don't you cry.
Chorus

I had a dream the other night,
When everything was still.
I thought I saw Susanna
A-comin' down the hill.
Chorus

The red, red rose was in her hand,
The tear was in her eye,
I said, "I come from Dixie Land,
Susanna, don't you cry."
Chorus

Chorus
Oh, Susanna!
Oh, don't you cry for me,
For I come from Alabama
With my banjo on my knee.

233

OH, YOU CAN'T GET TO HEAVEN

Oh, you can't get to heaven in a rocking chair
'Cause a rocking chair won't get you there
Oh, you can't get to heaven in a rocking chair
'Cause a rocking chair won't get you there
But I ain't gonna grieve, my Lord, no more
I ain't gonna grieve no more.

Oh, you can't get to heaven on roller skates
'Cause you'll roll right by St. Peter's gates
You can't get to heaven on roller skates
'Cause you'll roll right by St. Peter's gates
But I ain't gonna grieve, my Lord, no more
I ain't gonna grieve no more.

Oh, you can't get to heaven on a pair of skis
'Cause you'll schuss right through St. Peter's knees
You can't get to heaven on a pair of skis
'Cause you'll schuss right through St. Peter's knees
But I ain't gonna grieve, my Lord, no more
I ain't gonna grieve no more.

Oh, you can't get to heaven in (owner's name)'s car
'Cause _____'s car won't go that far
You can't get to heaven in _____'s car
'Cause _____'s car won't go that far
But I ain't gonna grieve, my Lord, no more
I ain't gonna grieve no more.

Oh, you can't get to heaven on a rocket ship
'Cause a rocket ship won't make the trip
You can't get to heaven on a rocket ship
'Cause a rocket ship won't make the trip
But I ain't gonna grieve, my Lord, no more
I ain't gonna grieve no more.

Oh, you can't get to heaven with Superman
'Cause our dear Lord is a Batman fan
You can't get to heaven with Superman
'Cause our dear Lord is a Batman fan
But I ain't gonna grieve, my Lord, no more
I ain't gonna grieve no more.

OLD MACDONALD

Old MacDonald had a farm, E-I-E-I-O!
And on his farm he had a cow, E-I-E-I-O!
With a moo-moo here, and moo-moo there,
Here a moo, there a moo, ev'rywhere a moo-moo,
Old MacDonald had a farm, E-I-E-I-O!

Old MacDonald had a farm, E-I-E-I-O!
And on his farm he had a pig, E-I-E-I-O!
With an oink-oink here, an oink-oink there,
Here an oink, there an oink, ev'rywhere an oink-oink,
Old MacDonald had a farm, E-I-E-I-O!

Old MacDonald had a farm, E-I-E-I-O!
And on his farm he had a duck, E-I-E-I-O!
With a quack-quack here, a quack-quack there,
Here a quack, there a quack, ev'rywhere a quack-quack,
Old MacDonald had a farm, E-I-E-I-O!

Old MacDonald had a farm, E-I-E-I-O!
And on his farm he had a horse, E-I-E-I-O~!
With a neigh-neigh here, a neigh-neigh there,
Here a neigh, there a neigh, ev'rywhre a neigh-neigh,
Old MacDonald had a farm, E-I-E-I-O!

(Continue adding your own animals, for instance:

Chickens: chick-chick
Donkey: hee-haw
Cat: meow-meow
Dog: bow-wow
Turkey: gobble-gobble)

OVER THE RIVER

Over the river and through the wood,
To grandmother's house we go!
The horse knows the way to carry the sleigh,
Through the white and drifted snow.

Over the river and through the wood,
Oh, how the wind does blow!
It stings the toes and bites the nose,
As over the ground we go.

Over the river and through the wood,
Trot fast, my dapple gray!
Spring over the ground like a hunting hound,
For this is Thanksgiving Day.

Over the river and through the wood,
Now grandfather's face I spy!
Hurray for the fun! Is the turkey done?
Hurray for the pumpkin pie!

(If you like, change the third verse's "this is Thanksgiving Day"
to "this is a special day." You could also change "turkey" and
"pumpkin pie" to reflect other seasons.)

237

POP GOES THE WEASEL

All around the cobbler's bench,
The money chased the weasel,
The monkey thought 'twas all in fun,
Pop, goes the weasel.

A penny for a spool of thread,
A penny for a needle,
That's the way the monkey goes,
Pop, goes the weasel.

The painter needs a ladder and brush,
The artist needs an easel,
The dancers need a fiddler's tune,
Pop, goes the weasel!

I've no time to wait or to sigh,
Or to tell the reason why,
Kiss me quick, I'm off, good-bye,
Pop, goes the weasel.

RISE AND SHINE

The Lord said to Noah, "There's gonna be a floody, floody"
The Lord said to Noah, "There's gonna be a floody, floody
Get those children out of the muddy, muddy"
Children of the Lord.
Chorus

So Noah he built them, he built them an arky, arky
Noah he built them, he built them an arky, arky
Built it out of hickory barky, barky
Children of the Lord.
Chorus

The animals they came on, they came on by twoseys, twoseys
Animals they came on, they came on by twoseys, twoseys
Elephants and kangarooseys, rooseys
Children of the Lord.
Chorus

It rained and poured for 40 dayseys, dayseys
Rained and poured for 40 dayseys, dayseys
Nearly drove those poor animals crazy, crazy
Children of the Lord.
Chorus

The sun came out and dried up the landy, landy
Sun came out and dried up the landy,landy
Everything was fine and dandy, dandy
Children of the Lord.

The animals they came off, they came off by twoseys, twoseys
Animals they came off, they came off by threesees, threesees
Elephants and chimpanzeesees, zeesees
Children of the Lord.
Chorus

Now this is the end of, the end of my story, story
This is the end of, the end of my story, story
Everything is hunky, dory, dory
Children of the Lord.
Chorus

Chorus:
Rise and shine, and sing out your glory, glory
Rise and shine, and sing out your glory, glory
Rise and shine, and sing out your glory, glory
Children of the Lord.

ROLL OVER

There were ten in the bed
And the little one said, "Roll over, Roll over."
So they all rolled over and one fell out -

There were nine in the bed
And the little one said, "Roll over, Roll over."
So they all rolled over and one fell out -

There were eight in the bed
And the little one said, "Roll over, Roll over."
So they all rolled over and one fell out -

There were seven in the bed
And the little one said, "Roll over, Roll over."
So they all rolled over and one fell out -

There were six in the bed
And the little one said, "Roll over, Roll over."
So they all rolled over and one fell out -

There were five in the bed
And the little one said, "Roll over, Roll over."
So they all rolled over and one fell out -

There were four in the bed
And the little one said, "Roll over, Roll over."
So they all rolled over and one fell out -

There were three in the bed
And the little one said, "Roll over, Roll over."
So they all rolled over and one fell out -

There were two in the bed
And the little one said, "Roll over, Roll over."
So they all rolled over and one fell out -

There was one in the bed
And the little one said,
"Good Night!"

ROW, ROW, ROW YOUR BOAT

Row, row, row your boat,
Gently down the stream.
Merrily, merrily, merrily, merrily,
Life is but a dream.

(This song is traditionally sung in rounds.)

SHE'LL BE COMIN' ROUND THE MOUNTAIN

She'll be comin' round the mountain when she comes,
She'll be comin' round the mountain when she comes,
She'll be comin' round the mountain,
She'll be comin' round the mountain,
She'll be comin' round the mountain when she comes.

She'll be drivin' six white horses when she comes,
She'll be drivin' six white horses when she comes,
She'll be drivin' six white horses,
She'll be drivin' six white horses,
She'll be drivin' six white horses when she comes,

Oh, we'll all go out to meet her when she comes,
Oh, we'll all go out to meet her when she comes,
Oh, we'll all go out to meet her,
Oh, we'll all go out to meet her,
Oh, we'll all go out to meet her when she comes.

Oh, we'll kill the old red rooster when she comes,
Oh, we'll kill the old red rooster when she comes,
Oh, we'll kill the old red rooster,
Oh, we'll kill the old red rooster,
Oh, we'll kill the old red rooster when she comes.

Oh, we'll all have chicken and dumplings when she comes,
Oh, we'll all have chicken and dumplings when she comes,
Oh, we'll all have chicken and dumplings,
Oh, we'll all have chicken and dumplings,
Oh, we'll all have chicken and dumplings when she comes.

We'll be singin' hallelujah when she comes,
We'll be singin' hallelujah when she comes,
We'll be singin' hallelujah,
We'll be singin' hallelujah,
We'll be singin' hallelujah when she comes.

SING YOUR WAY HOME

Sing your way home at the close of the day,
Sing your way home drive the shadows away,
Smile every mile for wherever you roam,
It will brighten your road,
It will lighten your load,
If you sing your way home.

THERE'S A HOLE IN THE BOTTOM OF THE SEA

There's a hole in the bottom of the sea.
There's a hole in the bottom of the sea.
There's a hole- there's a hole-
There's a hole in the bottom of the sea.

There's a log in the hole in the bottom of the sea.
There's a log in the hole in the bottom of the sea.
There's a log- there's a log-
There's a log in the hole in the bottom of the sea.

There's a bump on the log in the hole in the bottom of the sea.
There's a bump on the log in the hole in the bottom of the sea.
There's a bump- there's a bump-
There's a bump on the log in the hole in the bottom of the sea.

There's a frog on the bump on the log in the hole in the
    bottom of the sea.
There's a frog on the bump on the log in the hole in the
    bottom of the sea.
There's a frog- there's a frog-
There's a frog on the bump on the log in the hole in the
    bottom of the sea.

There's a wart on the frog on the bump on the log in the
    hole in the bottom of the sea.
There's a wart on the frog on the bump on the log in the
    hole in the bottom of the sea.
There's a wart- there's a wart-
There's a wart on the frog on the bump on the log in the
    hole in the bottom of the sea.

There's a hair on the wart on the frog on the bump on the
log in the hole in the bottom of the sea.
There's a hair on the wart on the frog on the bump on the
log in the hole in the bottom of the sea.
There's a hair- there's a hair-
There's a hair on the wart on the frog on the bump on the
log in the hole in the bottom of the sea.

There's a fly on the hair on the wart on the frog on the
bump on the log in the hole in the bottom of the sea.
There's a fly on the hair on the wart on the frog on the
bump on the log in the hole in the bottom of the sea.
There's a fly- there's a fly-
There's a fly on the hair on the wart on the frog on the
bump on the log in the hole in the bottom of the sea.

There's a speck on the fly on the hair on the wart on the
frog on the bump on the log in the hole in the bottom of
the sea.
There's a speck on the fly on the hair on the wart on the
frog on the bump on the log in the hole in the bottom of
the sea.
There's a speck- there's a speck
There's a speck on the fly on the hair on the wart on the
frog on the bump on the log in the hole in the bottom of
the sea!

THIS OLD MAN

This old man he played one
He played knick-knack on my thumb
Knick-knack, paddy-whack give a dog a bone
This old man came rolling home.

This old man he played two
He played knick-knack on my shoe
Knick-knack, paddy-whack give a dog a bone
This old man came rolling home.

This old man he played three
He played knick-knack on my knee
Knick-knack, paddy-whack give a dog a bone
This old man came rolling home.

This old man he played four
He played knick-knack on my door
Knick-knack, paddy-whack give a dog a bone
This old man came rolling home.

This old man he played five
He played knick-knack on my side
Knick-knack, paddy-whack give a dog a bone
This old man came rolling home.

This old man he played six
He played knick-knack on my sticks
Knick-knack, paddy-whack give a dog a bone
This old man came rolling home.

This old man he played seven
He played knick-knack up in heaven
Knick-knack, paddy-whack give a dog a bone
This old man came rolling home.

This old man he played eight
He played knick-knack on my gate
Knick-knack, paddy-whack give a dog a bone
This old man came rolling home.

This old man he played nine
He played knick-knack all the time
Knick-knack, paddy-whack give a dog a bone
This old man came rolling home.

This old man he played ten
He played knick-knack once again
Knick-knack, paddy-whack give a dog a bone
This old man came rolling home.

THREW IT OUT THE WINDOW

Little Jack Horner sat in a corner
Eating his Christmas pie-
He stuck in his thumb and pulled out a plum
And threw it out the window.
The window, the window
He threw it out the window
He stuck in his thumb and pulled out a plum
And threw it out the window!

Little Miss Muffet sat on a tuffet
Eating her curds and whey-
Along came a spider and sat down beside her
And threw it out the window!
The window, the window
He threw it out the window
Along came a spider and sat down beside her
And threw it out the window!

Little Bo Peep has lost her sheep
And doesn't know where to find them-
Leave them alone and they'll come home
And we'll throw them out the window
The window, the window
We'll throw them out the window
Leave them alone and they'll come home
And we'll throw them out the window!

Mary had a little lamb
Little lamb, little lamb-
Mary had a little lamb
And threw it out the window
The window, the window
She threw it out the window
Mary had a little lamb
And threw it out the window!

Old Mother Hubbard went to the cupboard
To find her poor dog a bone-
When she got there the cupboard was bare
So she threw it out the window
The window, the window
She threw it out the window
When she got there the cupboard was bare
So she threw it out the window!

Georgie Porgie pudding and pie
Kissed the girls and made them cry-
And when the boys began to play
He threw them out the window
The window, the window
He threw them out the window
And when the boys began to play
He threw them out the window!

Jack and Jill went up the hill
To fetch a pail of water-
And Jack fell down and broke his crown
And threw it out the window
The window, the window
He threw it out the window
And Jack fell down and broke his crown
And threw it out the window!

Little Boy Blue come blow your horn
The sheep's in the meadow, the cow's in the corn-
Is that the way you mind your sheep?
We'll throw them out the window
The window, the window
We'll throw them out the window
Is that the way you mind your sheep?
We'll throw them out the window!

THE WHEELS ON THE BUS

The wheels of the bus go round and round
Round and round, round and round.
The wheels of the bus go round and round
All through the town.

The wipers on the bus go swish, swish, swish,
Swish, swish, swish; swish, swish, swish
The wipers on the bus go swish, swish, swish,
All through the town.

The lights on the bus go blink, blink, blink
Blink, blink, blink; blink, blink, blink,
The lights on the bus go blink, blink, blink
All through the town.

The doors on the bus go open and shut
Open and shut, open and shut
The doors on the bus go open and shut
All through the town.

The money on the bus goes clink, clink, clink
Clink, Clink, clink; clink, clink, clink
The money on the bus goes clink, clink, clink
All through the town.

The driver on the bus says, "Move on back!
Move on back! Move on back!"
The driver on the bus says, "Move on back!"
All through the town.

The music on the bus goes la, la, la,
La, la, la; la, la, la
The music on the bus goes la, la, la
All through the town.

The people on the bus go up and down
Up and down, up and down.
The people on the bus go up and down
All through the town.

The horn on the bus goes honk, honk, honk
Honk, honk, honk; honk, honk, honk
The horn on the bus goes honk, honk, honk
All through the town.

The kids on the bus go yakkity-yak
Yakkity-yak, yakkity-yak
The kids on the bus go yakkity-yak
All through the town.

The driver on the bus says, "Quiet, please!
Quiet, please! Quiet, please!"
The driver on the bus says, "Quiet, please!"
All through the town.

The babies on the bus go wah, wah, wah,
Wah, wah, wah; wah, wah, wah
The babies on the bus go wah, wah, wah
All through the town.

The mothers on the bus go shh, shh, shh
Shh, shh, shh; shh, shh, shh
The mothers on the bus go shh, shh, shh
All through the town.

The wheels on the bus go round and round
Round and round, round and round
The wheels on the bus go round and round
All through the town.

(You can make up other verses to this song; add hand movements whenever you can).

WHO STOLE THE COOKIES FROM THE COOKIE JAR?

Who stole the cookies from the cookie jar?
David stole the cookies from the cookie jar.
Who me? Yes, you.
Not me. Then who?

Who stole the cookies from the cookie jar?
Christy stole the cookies from the cookie jar.
Who me? Yes, you.
Not me. Then who?

(Continue this game using family members' names.)

■ *FINGERPLAYS* ■

Fingerplays are loved by children, especially the little tykes. These little rhymes and movements often entertain children for long periods of time. Put a lot of character in your voice. You'll find lots of "bunny" fingerplays since they're such favorites.

EENCY WEENCY SPIDER

Eency weency spider climbed up the garden spout
(Fingers climb upward)
Down came the rain
(Wiggle fingers downward for rain)
And washed the spider out
(Push hands downward and outward)
Out came the sun
(Hands form a circle for the sun)
And dried up all the rain
Then eency weency spider climbed up the spout again.
(Fingers climb upward again)

251

THE MAN AND THE RABBIT

There was a little house in the middle of the wood
 (Make tips of fingers touching to form a roof)
And by the window a little man stood
 (Hold up one finger for the man)
He saw a rabbit hopping by
 (Bob two fingers up and down)
Knocking at the door.
 (Make a knocking motion)

"Help me! Help me! Help me!" he said
 (Throw up hands three times)
Or the hunter will shoot me dead
 (Make a gun with both hands)
Come little rabbit, come with me
 (Beckon with your hand)
Happy we will be.
 (Hold up two fingers and pet them with your other hand)

HERE IS BUNNY

Here is a bunny with his ears so funny
 (Hold two fingers up straight)
Here is his home in the ground
 (Index finger and thumb form a circle)
Up go his ears and he runs to his hole
 (With two fingers make quick bopping up and down motion)
When he hears a strange little sound!
 (Clap your hands)

LITTLE BUNNY FOO-FOO

Little Bunny Foo-Foo hopping through the forest
(Bob two fingers up and down)
Scooping up the field mice
(Make scooping motion with hand)
And bopping them on the head.
 (Make two fists and put down one fist on top of the other)

Down came the good fairy
(Wiggle two fingers in a downward motion)
And she said, "Little Bunny Foo-Foo I don't want to see you
scooping up the field mice and bopping them on the head.
(Shake index finger back and forth)
I'll give you three chances and if you don't behave, I'll turn you
into a goon."
 (Hold up three fingers)

The next day ... (Use the same finger actions except where noted)
Little Bunny Foo-Foo was hopping through the forest
Scooping up the field mice
And bopping them on the head.

Down came the good fairy
And she said, "Little Bunny Foo-Foo I don't want to see you
scooping up the field mice and bopping them on the head.
I'll give you two more chances and if you don't behave, I'll turn
you into a goon."
(Hold up two fingers)

The next day ...
Little Bunny Foo-Foo was hopping through the forest
Scooping up the field mice
And bopping them on the head.

Down came the good fairy
And she said, "Little Bunny Foo-Foo I don't want to see you
scooping up the field mice and bopping them on the head.
I'll give you one more chance and if you don't behave, I'll turn
you into a goon."
(Hold up one fingers)

The next day ...
Little Bunny Foo-Foo was hopping through the forest
Scooping up the field mice
And bopping them on the head.

Down came the good fairy
And she said, "I gave you three chances,
  (Hold up three fingers)
And you didn't behave, now you're a goon!"
  (Shake index finger back and forth)

(Moral of the story: Hare today, goon tomorrow!)

FIVE LITTLE BUNNIES

(Make hopping motions with fingers and hold up as many fingers as there are bunnies.)

Five little bunnies
Sitting by the door
One hopped away
And then there were four.

Four little bunnies
Sitting by a tree
One hopped away
And then there were three.

Three little bunnies
Looking at you
One hopped away
And then there were two.

Two little bunnies
Sitting in the sun
One hopped away
And then there was one.

One little bunny
Left all alone
He hopped away
And then there were none.

Bunnies, bunnies
Happy and gay
Bunnies, bunnies
Hop, hop, away!

FIVE LITTLE FROGGIES

This little froggy broke his toe
(Point to thumb)
This little froggy cried, "Oh, oh, oh!"
(Point to index finger)
This little froggy laughed and was glad
(Point to middle finger)
This little froggy cried and was sad
(Point to ring finger)
This little froggy, kind and good
(Point to little finger)
Hopped after the doctor as fast as he could.
(Little finger hops away)

TEN LITTLE INDIANS

(Hold up the appropriate number of fingers as the verse is sung.)

One little, two little, three little Indians
four little, five little, six little Indians
Seven little, eight little, nine little Indians
Ten little Indian boys.

(Then do the song in reverse.)

TEN LITTLE FINGERS

(Make actions as the words suggest.)

I have ten little fingers and they all belong to me.
I can make them do things,
Would you like to see?
I can close them up tight,
I can open them wide,
I can hold them up high,
I can hold them down low,
I can wave them to and fro,
And I can hold them just so.

WHERE IS THUMBKIN?

(Hold your hands behind your back. Reveal each finger as it occurs in the song, then return it behind your back. On the last verse bring out all the fingers, then return them behind your back.)

Where is Thumbkin? Where is Thumbkin?
Here am I, here am I.
How do you do this morning?
Very well, I thank you.
Run away, run away
Run away and play.
Continue using a different finger each time: pointer, tall man, ring finger, and pinky.
Where are all the fingers?

Where are all the fingers?
Here we are, here we are.
How do you do this morning?
Very well, we thank you.
Run away, run away
Run away and play.

HANDS ON SHOULDERS

(This is a good stretching exercise. Do the actions indicated.)

Hands on shoulders, hands on knees,
Put them behind you, if you please
Touch your shoulders, now your nose,
Now your hair, and now your toes
Put your hands up high in the air
Down at your sides, and touch your hair
Hands up high as before
Now clap you hands, one, two, three, four!

THE TURTLE

(Make actions as the words suggest.)

I have a little turtle who lives in the sand
He swims down in the water, and crawls up on the land
He snapped at a spider, and he snapped at a flea
He snapped at a minnow, and he snapped at me
He caught the spider, and he caught the flea
He caught the minnow, but he didn't catch me!

THE BEEHIVE

Here is the beehive
(Cup left hand down)
Where are the bees?
Hidden away where nobody sees.
 (Hide right hand fingers under left hand)
Soon they'll come creeping out of the hive
One, two, three, four, five.
 (Children count fingers that creep out one at a time)
Buzzzzzzzzz.

THE FINE FAMILY

This is mother so kind and dear
 (Close fist, raise thumb)
This is father so full of cheer
 (Raise pointer)
This is brother so straight and tall
 (Raise middle finger)
This is sister who plays with her doll
 (Raise ring finger)
This is baby, so sweet and small,
 (Raise pinkie)
See the family both great and small.
 (All fingers raised)

GOING TO BED

This little boy is going to bed
 (Place index finger in left hand)
Down on the pillow he lays his head
Wraps himself in the cover tight
 (Fold left hand over right index finger)
This is the way he sleeps all night.

Morning comes, he opens his eyes
 (Blink eyes like just waking up)
Back with a toss the cover flies
 (Open left fist)
Up he jumps, is dressed and away
Ready for work, ready for play.
(Quickly raise right finger and move it back and forth to make a
walking motion.)

POSSESSIONS

This is my book. It will open wide
 (Open both palms like a book)
To show the pictures that are inside.
This is my ball so big and round
 (Make a circle with both hands)
To toss in the air or roll on the ground.
Here's my umbrella to keep me dry
 (Use index finger in middle of cupped left hand)
When the raindrops fall from the sky.
This is my kitty. Just hear her purr
 (Right hand stroke left fist)
When I'm stroking her soft, warm fur.

HERE'S A BALL FOR BABY

(Make actions as the words suggest.)

Here's the ball for baby
Big and soft and round.
Here's the baby's hammer
Oh, how he can pound.

Here's the baby's music
Clapping, clapping so.
Here's the baby's soldiers
Standing in a row.

Here's the baby's trumpet
Toot, too-too-too-too-too.
Here's the way the baby
Plays at Peek-a-boo.

Here's the big umbrella
Keeps the baby dry.
Here's the baby's cradle
Rock-a-baby-bye.

CHAPTER 11

Coming Home

Coming Home

You've had a lovely trip, but now it's time to start back home. This is usually the hardest part of the trip. Most of the exciting events that everyone had looked forward to have happened. The anticipation that kept everyone happy on the way is now gone. For most of us the thought of being home in our own beds is a welcome thought, and yet that Monday-morning feeling that soon you'll be back in the same old routine puts a damper on the trip home. This chapter includes tips for making the return trip enjoyable and homecoming more hassle-free.

If you stayed with friends or relatives, review the lists you made before you left home (see Chapter 2). You'll be less likely to leave anything behind. If you stayed in motels or hotels, check the rooms before you leave. Look for clothes on a hook behind a door or mixed in the bedding, shoes under the bed, toiletries in the tub or shower, and food in the refrigerator. Checking will provide some peace of mind. You won't have to ask yourself, "Did we remember . . . ?" One time we stopped halfway home and ripped up half the car to see if we remembered the flashlight!

A sure way to ruin a trip is to rush home at breakneck speed. Sometimes it's necessary to cover some mileage, but the same guidelines for starting out on the road apply to going home again. The family needs stops to rest, eat and stretch. Without these breaks, everyone will be irritable and tired. Save a few toys and activities for the way home so you have interesting experiences in both directions. You might want to plan a different route home so you can stop at some new places.

The way back home provides a great perspective and opportunity for finishing the vacation journal or scrapbook. You can also make some notes on your packing lists or at the back of this book about experiences you've had on this trip that you want to remember for the next trip. Jot down what you would do differently, newly discovered scenic or time-saving routes, money-saving ideas, packing innovations, etc. You'd be surprised at how fast you'd otherwise forget these ideas.

■ *KEEPING THE MEMORIES* ■

Reminisce about the trip on the way home: the adventures you've had, your favorite meals, and your favorite experiences. Talk about what you've learned and how a new activity made you feel. (This is not the time to air grievances, however. End your vacation on a positive note.) A good game to help you remember what you've seen is "What Did I See?" Give descriptive clues of your various stops or experiences and let the kids guess and identify the places they have seen on the trip.

After you're home and settled in and the memories are still fresh, have a family get-together to talk about experiences on the trip. What were the highlights? What should you do differently next time? Show photographs, movies, or slides of the trip. This is a good time to label slide cases or videocassettes or record the date, place, and people on the back of photographs.

■ *HASSLE-FREE HOMECOMING* ■

Arriving home can be discouraging when you are met with all the unpacking, no food in the house, and no clean clothes. You will probably have a lot of laundry to do, and you may find it's easier to go to a laundromat to get it done quickly. If you left some basic food and baby supplies, a clean change of clothing, and a generally picked-up house, it won't seem so overwhelming.

It's a good idea to come home a day early from a long trip to give everyone a chance to unpack, unwind, and readjust before returning to work, school, and other activities.

■ *RETURN HOME CHECKLIST* ■

☐ Adjust heat or air conditioner or open windows

☐ Turn on any faucets you shut off

☐ Reset hot water thermostat

☐ Disconnect automatic light timers

☐ Reconnect appliances

☐ Turn icemaker back on

☐ Adjust bell on phone/play back answering machine messages

- ☐ Water plants

- ☐ Inspect house

- ☐ Notify the people taking care of your home/collect keys

- ☐ Unpack and put away luggage, food, clothing, equipment

- ☐ Clean up gear: cooking, luggage, equipment

- ☐ Do laundry

- ☐ Restart milk/food/water deliveries

- ☐ Collect mail from post office, neighbor, or friend

- ☐ Restart newspaper delivery or collect papers from neighbor or friend

- ☐ Get pet from kennel, friend, or family member

- ☐ Move outdoor furniture, equipment, valuables back where they belong

- ☐ Car: wash, clean interior, windows, resupply, unpack, take off special racks

- ☐ Restock picnic box, toiletries, wallet

- ☐ Summer: take care of yard/ Winter: shovel snow

☐ Take clothes to cleaners

☐ Take film to be developed

☐ Go to bank: make deposits, withdrawals, cash in traveler's checks, exchange foreign currency, get valuables from safe-deposit box

☐ Shop for food and household supplies

☐ Call family and friends

☐ Update and finish trip journal, notes, mount pictures

☐ Write thank-you notes

☐ Give gifts to family, friends, neighbors

☐ Read mail and newspapers

Index

B

E
Eating in the car, 102-3
Eating schedules, 103-4
Entertaining children, at hotel/motel, 67-68
Entertaining children, at restaurant, 110-11

F
Family council, 3, 130, 142, 265
Fares, children's airplane, 86
Fares, children's train, 98
Feeding the baby, 112-13
Ferries, 11
Finances, 13-18
Fingerplays, 251-61
  Beehive, The, 259
  Eency Weency Spider, 251
  Fine Family, The, 259
  Five Little Bunnies, 255
  Five Little Froggies, 256
  Going To Bed, 260
  Hands On Shoulders, 258
  Here Is Bunny, 252
  Here's A Ball For Baby, 261
  Little Bunny Foo-Foo, 253
  Man and the Rabbit, The, 252
  Possessions, 260
  Ten Little Fingers, 257
  Ten Little Indians, 256
  Turtle, The, 258
  Where is Thumbkin?, 257

Heat exhaustion, 122-23
Homecoming, hassle-free, 267
Homework, trip, 9-11
Hotels, 12-13
Hypothermia, 124-25

I
Identification tags, 87-89, 132
Itinerary, 18

J
Jetlag, 96
Journal, vacation, 168, 265

K
Keeping the memories, 265
Keys, misplaced, 133

L
Lap tray, 158-59
Laundry, 37
License plate games, 186-87
Limited action games, 206-7
Lost car keys, 133
Lost children, 88, 131-32
Lost items, accommodations, 68, 264
Lost wallets, 132
Luggage, airline, 88-90
Luggage tags, 88-89

M
Meals, airline, 92-94
Meals, train, 98-99

Plastic bags, 43-44
Playpens, 38
Postcards, 17, 20
Potty, portable, 78
Preparation, trip, 18-20
Prescriptions, 20, 37, 116-17
Private time, 5
Protection, car, 133-34
Public, kids in, 148

Q
Quiet games, 208-9
Quiet time, 5, 76

R
Reading material, 37
Records, trip, 16
Recreational vehicle, 11
Relatives, staying with, 68-69
Reservations, accommodations, 13, 66-67
Reservations, airplane, 84-86, 91
Responsibilities, children's, 152
Restaurants, 19, 108-12
Restrooms, airplane, 94
Restroom use, 78
Rest stops, 72-75
Rewards, 153

S
Safety, 129-34
Safety, accommodations, 67
Sand toys, 79

Transportation, 11-12
Travel agents, 84
Travelers checks, 14

V
Valuable items, 36-37

W
Waiting games, 209-10
Wallets, lost or stolen, 132
Wardrobe planning, 34-35
Water, beach use, 80
Water, drinking, 108
Word games, 192-201
Wrinkled clothing, 37, 40-41
Wrist handholder, 79, 87, 131

About the Author

Arlene Kay Butler lives in Agoura Hills, California with her husband and five children, who range from toddler to teen. When not traveling with her family, she is a home-management consultant, lecturer, and writer (most recently, of a book about holiday parties).

Notes:

Notes: